SOUTINE

FRONTISPIECE: *Man in a Green Coat*. c.1921. Oil, 34⅞ x 21¾".
Collection Mr. and Mrs. Samuel A. Marx, Chicago

SOUTINE

BY MONROE WHEELER

THE MUSEUM OF MODERN ART   NEW YORK

IN COLLABORATION WITH THE CLEVELAND MUSEUM OF ART

REPRINT EDITION, 1966   PUBLISHED FOR
THE MUSEUM OF MODERN ART BY ARNO PRESS

CONTENTS

ACKNOWLEDGMENTS

On behalf of the Trustees of The Museum of Modern Art and The Cleveland Museum of Art I wish to extend grateful acknowledgment for invaluable counsel and collaboration to the lenders listed below and to the following: Jean-Pierre Brasseur, M. and Mme Marcellin Castaing, Raymond Cogniat, C. C. Cunningham, Udo Einsild, Jacques Guérin, Gaston de Havenon, Eardley Knollys, André Lejard, Jacques Lipchitz, M. Mouradian, François Reichenbach, Georges Renand, Sam Salz, Albert Skira, James Thrall Soby, Charles Sterling, Jacques Wertheimer, Glenway Wescott.

MONROE WHEELER

LENDERS TO THE EXHIBITION

Mr. and Mrs. Lee A. Ault, New York; Dr. and Mrs. Harry Bakwin, New York; Mme Germaine Bignou, Paris; Mr. and Mrs. Leigh B. Block, Chicago; Dr. Harry Austin Blutman, New York; Arthur Bradley Campbell, Palm Beach, Fla.; William E. Campbell, Mobile, Ala.; M. and Mme Marcellin Castaing, Lèves, Eure-et-Loire, France; Miss Pamela T. Colin, New York; Mr. Ralph F. Colin, Jr., New York; Mr. and Mrs. Ralph F. Colin, New York; Richards H. Emerson, New York; Paul Gardner, Kansas City, Mo.; Miss Adelaide Milton de Groot, New York; Jacques Guérin, Paris; Leonard C. Hanna, Jr., Cleveland, Ohio; Mr. and Mrs. Sidney Janis, New York; Mrs. H. Harris Jonas, New York; Mr. and Mrs. Albert D. Lasker, New York; Mr. and Mrs. Sam A. Lewisohn, New York; Frederic R. Mann, Philadelphia, Pa.; Mr. and Mrs. Samuel A. Marx, Chicago; Henri Matisse, Paris; Mr. and Mrs. Oscar Miestchaninoff, New York; Mr. and Mrs. Clifford Odets, New York; Henry Pearlman, New York; Jack I. Poses, New York; Bernard Reichenbach, Paris; François Reichenbach, Paris; Mr. and Mrs. Bernard Reis, New York; Mr. and Mrs. Edward G. Robinson, Beverly Hills, Calif.; Mme Jean Walter, Paris; Mrs. Lloyd Bruce Wescott, Clinton, N. J.; Mr. and Mrs. Harry Lewis Winston, Birmingham, Mich.

The Albright Art Gallery, Buffalo, New York; The Art Institute of Chicago, Chicago; Kunstmuseum, Lucerne, Switzerland; The Phillips Gallery, Washington, D. C.; The Portland Art Museum, Portland, Ore.

9

Chaim Soutine

1894 *   Born in Smilovitchi, near Minsk, Western Russia

1910   Vilna; School of Fine Arts for three years

1913   Arrived in Paris. Ecole des Beaux-Arts, Atelier Cormon. Lived at Cité Falguière

1916   Studio in *La Ruche,* "The Beehive," Rue Dantzig. Met Lipchitz, Modigliani, Zborowsky

1918   First brief visit to Cagnes

1919   Leaves *La Ruche.* First visit to Ceret

1920–22 Ceret, Paris, Cagnes, but mostly Ceret. Returned to Paris with 200 paintings

1923   Paris. Pictures bought by Albert C. Barnes. Two months at Cagnes. First predominantly white pictures

1924   Paris, Cagnes. First success

1925   Paris, Cagnes. Rue du Mont St. Gothard, Avenue du Parc Montsouris

1926   Paris. Rue de l'Aude

1927   Paris. Vacations at Blanc, Indre. Painted dead fowl and other still life

1928   Paris. Avenue du Parc Montsouris

1929   Paris. Chatel Guyon. Painted *valets-de-chambres*

1930   Paris. Passage d'Enfer. Illness. Convalescence at Nice

1931–35 Paris. Traveled continuously. Summers at Chateau de Lèves, near Chartres

1935   First major exhibition, The Arts Club of Chicago

1936–37 Paris. Avenue d'Orléans

1938–39 Paris. Villa Seurat

1940   Paris. Civry. Refuses invitation to go to America

1941–43 Champigny sur Veuldre, Indre-et-Loire

1943   Died, Paris. Buried in Montparnasse Cemetery

1945   Memorial Exhibition, Galerie de France, Paris

* Soutine's birthdate of 1893, in contradiction to the previously accepted 1894, has lately been established by M. Pierre Courthion.

OPPOSITE: *Red Gladioli*. c.1919. Oil, 21 ½ x 18".
Collection Mr. and Mrs. Harry Lewis Winston, Birmingham, Mich.

OPPOSITE: *Fowl with Tomatoes.* 1925-26. Oil, 39½ x 17¾".
Collection Bernard Reichenbach, Paris

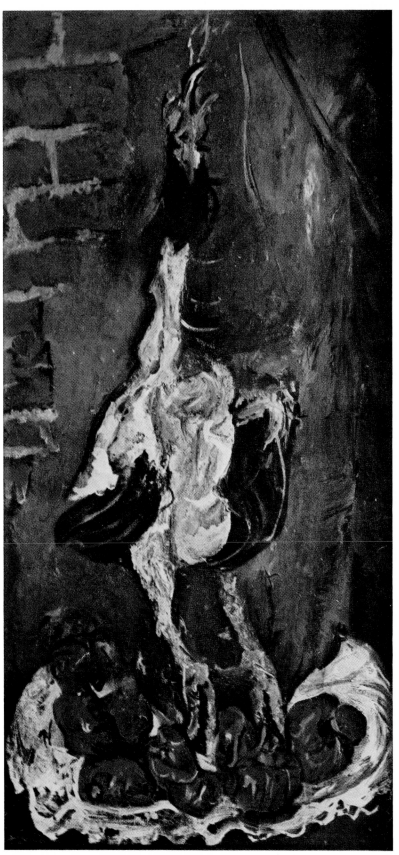

OPPOSITE: *Carcass of Beef.* 1926. Oil, 45¾ x 31⅞".
Collection Mme Germaine Bignou, Paris

OPPOSITE: *The Pastry Cook*. c.1927. Oil, 30⅛ x 27¼".
Collection Mr. and Mrs. Lee A. Ault, New York

OPPOSITE: *Seated Choir Boy.* c.1930. Oil on wood, 25¼ x 14¼".
Private collection, Paris

OPPOSITE: *Chartres Cathedral.* 1933. Oil on wood, 36 x 19½″.
Collection Mrs. Lloyd Bruce Wescott, Clinton, N. J.

SOUTINE

Soutine, Pascin, Utrillo and Modigliani — they have been grouped together as though violence of temper and proneness to trouble constituted a school of art. In France they are called *les peintres maudits* — painters under a curse. The lives of some Post-Impressionists, notably Gauguin and van Gogh, have put in the general mind and in the repertory of journalism about art, a concept of melodramatic greatness. Here was another such generation.

Modigliani, even in the year of his death, drugged and debilitated, kept his extraordinary facility, and never departed from his same felicitous type of picture until the end. Pascin indulged his sensuality and wild, cynical humor until it turned to despair, then resolutely cut his life short; he did not linger over it to say what it meant. Utrillo's alcoholism and illness were a living death for many years; but he has risen from it, and goes on painting in blissful simplicity.

Soutine was the least calamitous and least dissipated of the four, but perhaps the saddest. For as his art developed, it offered no distraction from his anxieties, animosities and self-reproach — no escape. Not that he intended any effect of autobiography by means of his art. But from an early age he used his hardship, pessimism and truculence to set a tragic tone for his painting, irrespective of its subject matter. Limiting the themes of his work to conventional categories — still life, landscape, portraiture and picturesque figure-painting — he would always charge his pictures with extreme implications of what he had in mind: violence of nature, universality of hunger, and a peculiar mingling of enthusiasms and antipathies.

Which came first? Did his art sadden him so that it cast an irremediable shadow on his way of life? Or was his experience of life so grievous that his art could express nothing but grief and bitterness? It seemed a vicious circle. In any case, instead of relieving his mind, the intense seriousness of his artistic effort only dug deeper the melancholy channels of his thought.

But in his work as a mature artist there is an entire range of his reactions to tragic themes which is not tragic at all. It is instead exuberant and joyous. For Soutine was highly sensitive to the dramatic contrasts and clashes in humanity and nature,

The Artist's Studio, Cité Falguière. 1915.
Oil, 25½ x 19½". Private collection, New York

not only life versus death, good versus evil, but also wealth versus poverty and elemental forces versus conventions. And whenever his work went well, he had a wildly excited sense of the strength of his own personality transcending them.

Chaim Soutine was born in 1894[*] in Smilovitchi, a sombre village of wooden houses twelve miles from Minsk, in the Lithuanian part of Western Russia. He was the tenth of eleven children of a miserably poor Jewish tailor who wanted him to become a shoemaker.

But he was a born painter. In later years he recalled his infant delight in the vari-colored effects of sunlight on the wall beside his bed, before he was able to talk. At the age of seven, he so desired a colored pencil that he stole some utensils from his mother's kitchen in order to buy one, and was punished by two days incarceration in the family cellar. Sometimes in rebellion against the family life, with so many elder brothers and sisters in small quarters, he would run away and sleep in neighboring farm buildings or in the fields. He was an inattentive, unsatisfactory student, and at one point was expelled from school.

But by the time he was sixteen he had begun to be an artist. He made friends with a simpleton of the village and produced a likeness of him. He then had the temerity to ask the rabbi to pose for his portrait. The rabbi's son, feeling that his father had

[*] Soutine's birthdate of 1893, in contradiction to the previously accepted 1894, has lately been established by M. Pierre Courthion.

been insulted, met him at the door and beat him so brutally that it took him a week to recover. His mother threatened to bring suit and was appeased by a contribution of twenty-five roubles toward her son's education. With this sum of money he set out for Minsk to study painting, accompanied by another boy of the village, Michel Kikoine. Their first teacher was a man named Krueger who guaranteed success after a three-months' course.

A little later the two aspirants went on to the School of Fine Arts in Vilna; at first Soutine failed in the entrance requirements, but one of the teachers gave him private instruction and he was admitted, and followed the school's courses for three years. A friendly doctor of Vilna contributed something to his support, and in 1913 helped him to make the great journey to Paris, where he found Kikoine, and another fellow student of Vilna, Pinchus Kremegne.

He enrolled in Fernand Cormon's class at the Ecole des Beaux-Arts where van Gogh and Toulouse-Lautrec had also studied; but this further academic opportunity seems not to have given him satisfaction. Before long he established himself independently on the Left Bank, at first in a humble studio in the Cité Falguière (opposite). Here he began to work out his artistic salvation, very slowly, with changes of mind as to his manner and subject matter, in dire poverty. Later he moved to an old building transformed into studios, in the Rue Dantzig known as *La Ruche,* "The Beehive," where Chagall, Kisling, and other artists lived.

Soutine was never a very sociable or friendly man, but at this time he became acquainted with Laurens, Cendrars, Pascin, Lipchitz, Miestchaninoff, Coubine and Zadkine. None of them appear to have influenced him especially, but Lipchitz introduced him to Modigliani, and Modigliani brought his work to the attention of the perceptive and courageous dealer, Leopold Zborowski.

We have an excellent self-portrait painted when he was about twenty-three years old (p. 34): a raw-boned, truculent but sensitive youth whom anyone who knew him in his mature years would instantly recognize. Modigliani painted him twice, with a more brooding and peaceful face than in his own portrayal (p. 35). In the late twenties, when the writer first saw him, he was pale and slender, hypochondriacal, and under doctor's orders as to his food and drink.

Elie Faure, though dwelling at length upon Soutine's Jewish origin (bibl. 13), said that he looked rather Slavic, more like a Kalmuk or a Tartar, and that the most constant of his moods was the characteristically Slavic "longing for things too changeable or flexible to lay hands on." The expressions of his face varied a great deal, sullen or suspicious, timorous or arrogant, but upon occasion as friendly as a child's. A man of slight stature, he moved in an uneasy or evasive way, a little one-sidedly. His small and delicate hands suggested a more meticulous way of painting than he ever practised. Occasionally he took pains to be well dressed, but his clothes soon became shabby and dirty. At the end of his life his cheeks grew hollow, his full lips drooped with a

Self Portrait. c.1917. Oil, 18 x 21½". Collection Henry Pearlman, New York

Modigliani: *Portrait of Soutine.* 1917.
Oil, 36¼ x 23¼". The Chester Dale Collection.
Photo courtesy The Philadelphia
Museum of Art.

suggestion of boredom or bitterness, but when he spoke his black eyes still glittered with romanticism about himself and his art.

The orthodox faith of his forefathers seems never to have meant very much to him. In his mature years in France he suffered no anti-Semitic persecution nor even any notable injustice on that account. But he did feel an exalted self-consciousness as a Jew and a sense of historic import in his migration from Eastern Europe to the world capital.

More painting has been done in France in this century by immigrants from Eastern European ghettos than the Jewish nation has produced in all the centuries gone by. Whether by their own religious traditions, or by the repressions and injustices of others, Jews had previously been kept out of the arts almost entirely. Suddenly, there they were in the vanguard, uprooted but quickly digging in everywhere, mixing in everything, playing a great role in civilization. It may be that for Soutine and for other of his fellow artists in Paris, the important thing was not the sense of race

35

Still Life with Soup Tureen.
c.1916. Oil, 24 x 29″. Collection
Mr. and Mrs. Ralph F. Colin,
New York

repression but the opposite, the rapidity of liberation — what we now call vertical social mobility — and its consequences, psychological and otherwise. It made them bold, even insolent, concentrated upon their advancement, indefatigable; but it kept them under continuous strain, ever insecure and perhaps incredulous. Those days of their youth seemed too good to be true.

Soutine's career, notwithstanding the loneliness and penury of the beginning, was a success story. By the time he was thirty-five, the whole world of art had heard of him, and there was a ready market for anything he cared to paint. To any of his family in Smilovitchi this would have seemed a miracle; and so it did to Soutine himself. But he always thought of himself as a wanderer and an Ishmael, no matter how successful. He expected the worst of everyone, even of himself. And in all his extraordinary and implausible life, he achieved no real self-assurance, no comfort or any great illusion except about art. When his life-story drew to an untimely close, with the various hindrances to his painting, isolation and fright during the war, it must have come as no great surprise to him.

All those young foreign artists in Paris had one thing in common. They were high-minded. They had come there to seek their fortune by means of art, but on the other hand they declared, and as a rule seriously meant, that art was to come first, before fortune. If they failed of celebrity and worldly recompense, they would fall back on the prepared position of "art for art's sake": disbelief of critics, suspicion of dealers, contumely for collectors. But almost to a man they were sincere. Having left religions behind them with their various family affections and customs of childhood, they now brought to the pursuit of art a kind of religiosity. Soutine was a less gregarious man than most, with nothing Messianic about him; no leadership, no eloquence. But it did seem to him inevitable, perhaps suitable and agreeable, that he should be somewhat martyred for his art. There were times when he seemed to insist on maladjustment with his fellow men, to relish hostility, and to prefer distress.

Zborowski, his dealer, said that France was paradise for Soutine because it was a place where he could sit on a park bench and not be ordered away by a policeman. When he wore no hat, and Zborowski remonstrated with him, he replied with rare humor, "I can't go around like the Tsar every day." Such petty details of his youth in France were the subject of Soutine's own conversation in later years, no less than of his friends and admirers. He made a legend of his personal life, or rather a series of legends, boasting of all his mishaps, his hardships, and peculiarities of his character. He was afraid of coming to be like other men, and losing his singularity as an artist, his potency and magic. He also believed that a painter should stay poor, at least should

Still Life with Chair. 1916–17.
Oil, 29 x 21½". Collection
Dr. Harry Austin Blutman, New York

never settle down with savings and a regular income. Now and then, when he made considerable sums of money, he apparently took pleasure in getting rid of it, reverting as quickly as he could to the *status quo ante*. Part of this may have been a real taste for disorder and squalor, but part of it was his mysterious reverence for himself just as he was at the time when his talent first made itself manifest.

With all this he had an unappeasable dislike and mistrust of middle-class ways, middle-class personal relationships and business practices. To convince him of one's true admiration, one had to keep absolute fidelity, and not have any of his rivals' work. None of his collectors, even the most enthusiastic and exclusive, quite succeeded in persuading him that their principle interest might not be to resell at the earliest opportunity and make a profit. On the other hand, mere benevolence seemed to undermine his independence. It seemed beneath his dignity as a man of the people and as an artist of consequence, to accept kindnesses.

One of the anecdotes through which we can most clearly glimpse him is Marcellin Castaing's account of their first meeting. He and his wife had just begun to take an interest in modern art, investigating the new reputations and buying a little. Modigliani recommended his young friend from Smilovitchi and told them that he needed help. Soutine was too shy to meet them indoors and gave them a rendezvous on the sidewalk in front of a café. There they found him pacing up and down, unprepossess-

Still Life with Fish. c.1917. Oil, 16 x 25″. Collection Miss Adelaide Milton de Groot, New York

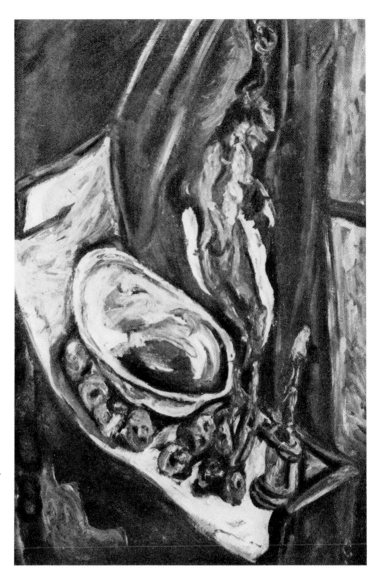

Still Life with Pheasant. c.1918.
Oil, 35½ x 23″. Collection
Frederic R. Mann, Philadelphia, Pa.

sing, overwrought, not at all friendly, with a canvas under his arm. M. Castaing was
impressed by his work, there under the streetlight, but wanted to come to the studio
where there might be a greater number of pictures to choose from, and offered him
an advance of one hundred francs. Soutine would have none of it; "You don't like
my painting, you only want to help me. If you had given me one franc for my picture
I would have taken it." Then he stalked away by himself and the Castaings saw
nothing more of him for many years.

Perhaps no man ever was more greatly and effectively befriended by various art-
loving women, distinguished in their several ways. But his disbelief in respectability,
his horror of feeling honorbound or dutybound to anyone (art had to be his one and

only bondage) made him upon occasion unfriendly and even reprehensible in his dealings with them. They seemed more bourgeois than men; comfort-loving, security-seeking, clinging, dangerous to the dedicated and embattled artist. In all his affections there was an admixture of pity; and pity of women led to entanglement and the desire not to be entangled inspired in him resentment and cruelty.

There is a terrible tale of one unfortunate woman, coming in all honesty with a claim upon him. But he did not think her honest, or perhaps suffered so frantic a dread of responsibility toward her that his thoughts did not function at all normally. He raged at her and refused and refused. At last, to make the refusal the more final, he showed her some thousand franc notes which he could have given her but would not, then threw them in the fireplace and burned them before her eyes.

His love of painting, his morality of painting gave him (as in the case of Gauguin) an excuse for any such ruthlessness. His sense of vocation made him pitiless. On the other hand, painting also served as penance and atonement. But he was neither a dull nor a complacent man, and now and then, in his portraits of evidently heartbroken, over-submissive or hard-bitten women, he may have been referring to harm he himself had done.

Soutine said that in his early days in Paris, as long as he painted in a reasonably conventional or decorative style, he had no difficulty selling enough to support him-

Reclining Woman. 1917. Oil, 23¼ x 36½″. Private collection, New York

View of Montmartre. c.1919. Oil, 25¾ x 32″. Collection William E. Campbell, Mobile, Ala.

self. Was this a boast, or was it bitter irony? He came to Paris in 1913; we do not hear of a dealer advancing him money until 1919, or of a collector buying any amount of his work until 1923. Ten years! — in which, if a youngster has to live by his brush, he must produce an immense number of canvases. Be this as it may, the hardship and jeopardy he must have endured in that decade are scarcely imaginable nowadays. He admitted to his friend, Udo Einsild, that he once was driven by hunger to commit a theft of bottles which he exchanged for bread, even as at Smilovitchi he had stolen kitchen utensils to procure his first colored pencil. But somehow he managed. There are ups and downs in the lives of all such opportunist young men which they themselves can scarcely comprehend a few years later; and whoever is up will help his friends who are down. We know that, on occasion, Modigliani, though ten years older and already celebrated, came and slept on Soutine's floor, and afterward told of how the bedbugs tormented him until he removed all his clothes and poured water in a magic circle on the floor around him. One of the earliest descriptive references to

Landscape with Church Tower. c.1919. Oil, 21⅛ x 28¾″. Collection Henry Pearlman, New York

Soutine's way of painting also came from Modigliani's lips. By that time the latter was gravely addicted to drugs, as well as alcohol, and as he was commencing a bout of intoxication he remarked, "Everything dances around me as in a landscape by Soutine."

There are certain references to Soutine's drinking to excess in his youth. But he soon had to discipline himself against any such indulgence. He always suffered from chronic nervous indigestion. This was probably engendered by the irregular and insufficient nourishment of his boyhood, and surely aggravated by every trait of his psychology. This condition developed into a series of stomach ulcers so that, to avoid pain, what he ate and drank soon became a matter of extreme concern to him. And, characteristically, he made his abstemiousness a matter of morality as well as therapy, a kind of puritanism for art's sake, and took pride in it. Declining to drink, instead of referring to his health, he would say, "No, I must not let myself be corrupted."

For Soutine never forgot that he had come to Paris to paint like the masters he idolized. In the early years he talked mainly of Tintoretto and El Greco. His enthu-

View of Ceret. c.1919. Oil, 21¼ x 28¾". Kunstmuseum, Lucerne, Switzerland

siasm for Rembrandt developed a little later. He professed not to like van Gogh, but it seems evident that van Gogh's late Provençal landscapes must have emboldened him in his early approach to both landscape and portraiture.

However, the detection and expounding of the influences which contribute to the formation of a young artist's style is not one of the branches of art scholarship which can be made very exact. He may study for years with a famous master, but it may be some reproduction in a periodical, or a casual conversation in a café with a friend, perhaps not even an artist, which may give him the cue to his own important message and latent originality.

Soutine must surely have been acquainted with German expressionism. He knew Chagall, who had appeared in German magazines, along with Ensor, Corinth, Nolde, Schmidt-Rottluff and Kokoschka. And the boldness and extreme colorfulness of *Les Fauves* must not have escaped his attention. But to counterbalance this, we see how

The Hill. c.1919. Oil, 29 x 21¾". Collection Mr. and Mrs. Sidney Janis, New York

Village Square. c.1920. Oil, 29⅞ x 33¾″. Collection Henry Pearlman, New York

Soutine responded delightedly to certain promptings of the work of one of the most intensely French painters of the century, Bonnard, as in his early *Still Life with Chair* (p. 37). For Paris, in the opinion of Eastern and Central Europeans as well as Frenchmen, was the capital of world art, and all these gifted young art-immigrants thought of themselves as Parisians. Whatever traditions of their native lands they may have brought with them, they were never entirely happy to be regarded by French critics as profound primitives or thrilling barbarians.

In the earliest work of Soutine which has been preserved, he showed neither a marked academic facility nor any decisive revolutionary purpose. His development was more a matter of intuitive gestation than of deliberate innovation or experiment. As a matter of course, in the art school at Vilna, and at the Beaux-Arts under Cormon, he was taught a kind of nineteenth-century realism, dark and painstaking. There is something of this to be seen in the *Still Life with Soup Tureen* (p. 36), a rather awkwardly formal arrangement enhanced by luminous whites and warm shadows. *The Spotted Vase* with its yellow flower, a year or so later, seems less conscious of modernism, with a discernible influence of Matisse. His dramatic treatment of fish and fowl appears first in the serpentine *Still Life with Fish* (p. 38) in which we see the Soutine of later years powerfully foreshadowed. The great mouth gapes, almost gasps. The eye protrudes in fearful intensity — the dead forms as vigorous on the slanting table as in their wild existence under water. Then came the *Still Life with Pheasant* (p. 39), slender bird, suspended over a pattern of apples on a marble table top; and the *Brace of Pheasants* with the sunshiny yellow cloth under them. All are simply youthful Parisian work, not for all their vigor indicative of a very forceful temperament or great spirit of innovation. Brilliantly executed as to brushwork, the *Reclining Woman* (p. 40) is his first successful attempt to render the large areas of white which he was to carry to greater perfection in the great figure paintings ten years later. In all these *La Ruche* works one perceives only the commencement of the emotional intensity which was soon to follow.

Another subject which preoccupied him for a while at *La Ruche* was gladioli (color plate p. 13). He painted several canvases of more or less the same vaseful, and the point of his fascination and research in them all seems to have been the play of thick but sinuous stems and flaring red blossoms. It may not have been so much the true forms of the leaves and petals which appealed to him as the blood-redness, fire-redness, which he rendered like little licking flames.

This sinuousness, like wind-whipped plumage, struck his imagination in other ways. One of his first notable landscapes is the *View of Montmartre* (p. 41), evocative and strong, with its pagoda-like buildings. The trees show the first use of the fine dense emerald greens that, no less than scarlet and mother-of-pearl, were to become synonymous with his name. Closely related to this is the vigorous *Landscape with Church Tower* (p. 42), in which we observe a singularity that was to recur frequently in his

Red Roofs, c.1920. Oil, 32 x 25½″. Collection Henry Pearlman, New York

View of the Village. c.1921. Oil, 28¾ x 38″. Private collection, New York

work for a number of years — everything violently inclines to the right. In the great case of El Greco there was a somewhat similar trait, a twisted perpendicularity in canvas after canvas, and some critics on Spanish art have suggested that it may have derived from a disorder of eyesight. The slanting landscapes of Soutine might be explained in some such way, but if the trouble was optical, he was presently to recover from it.

In 1928, Waldemar George (bibl. 16) pointed out that the shock of Soutine's way of painting was not so much a matter of form, deformation and malformation, as a certain wildness of rhythm loosed on the canvas, twisting in every lineament of nature and human nature; "It bends and shakes his figures as though they had St. Vitus' dance. Harmonious still lifes, flowers and fruits, it reduces to rags and tatters. Houses oscillate on their foundations and move ardently hither and thither in the landscape, turning it topsy-turvy as in a series of seismic shocks." These sentences of clever syn-

Gnarled Trees. c.1921. Oil, 28¾ x 36¼″. Collection Mr. and Mrs. Ralph F. Colin, New York

thesis referred to Soutine's fully mature work, but we may note that as early as 1919 in paintings done in Paris and in Cagnes on the French Riviera he had broached the main themes of his life work and strongly hinted at his later styles.

In this year Zborowski, now developing a serious interest in him, proposed his going to a small town in the Pyrenees called Ceret, where he stayed the greater part of the next three years.

The vehement and idiosyncratic style that he developed there shocked all of Soutine's contemporaries, and we still feel a strong impact and some confusion as we look at it today. It is as though this young man of thirty years ago felt that he had a world-shaking message.

The landscapes of the Pyrenees seem, indeed, to be shaken by some cosmic force; the architecture becomes flexible and billows like a canvas, the trees reel and stumble about, and the colors seem to have been wrested hungrily from the spectrum; his palette seemed to enter the dance with his forms, the color of one thing whirling away with the form of another.

Was Soutine at this time what might be called an abstract expressionist? In the blue and yellow *Village Square* (p. 45), the actual representation of the hill town contributes little to our enjoyment, but we see that it contributed greatly to Soutine's inspiration. What inspired him was the configuration of the external world, though none of the details contributory to verisimilitude impressed him very much. In exuberant celebration of the natural forms, he developed upon his canvas supernatural jewel-like pigments and arbitrary rugged textures, and carried the over-all pattern so far that we scarcely know or care what it represents. But it expresses what inspired it with a force of emotion stronger than most abstract canvases. It may be that emotions can only be strongly expressed with allusion to some view of external reality, and that no matter how far the painter departs from it, he can still convey a greater impact of emotion than in a work disconnected from specific subject matter. But in any case, for Soutine, the communication of feeling in which he excels must speak of what he has experienced, whether or not he can make this communication clear.

The three years from 1919 to 1922, spent for the most part at Ceret, were the most prolific of his life; during this time he painted over two hundred canvases. His accelerated production has been attributed to his alarm at the death of his friend Modigliani, who died in 1920 at the height of his career, ruined by dissipation and distress. The suicide of Modigliani's young wife during the funeral gave it a note of Greek tragedy amid the aspirations of the studios and the frivolities of the cafés. The calamitous extinguishment of this artist of greater facility and more fortunate background must have caused all of his friends to doubt the feasibility of their wild, artistic way of life, and it is possible that the emotions precipitated by this event expressed themselves in certain tumultuous and obscure canvases which Soutine did at the time.

During this significant phase of his career he appears, above all, to have been seeking

The Haunted House, Ceret. 1921–22. Oil, 31 x 34″. Collection Dr. Harry Austin Blutman, New York

a new style. And the real tragedies in his mind were those of the striving of art, with tragic excesses of zeal, and unreasonable degrees of dejection when the work miscarried. His previous work, although in a style which seems to verge upon that of his maturity, disappointed him; otherwise he would have gone on with it.

Of all the phases of Soutine's painting, this is the least legible, the hardest to understand, and the most rapid in experimental transitions. The sombre, interspersed colors of the Ceret pictures, the upheavals of ambiguous and repetitious form, constituted a tremendous experiment, a determined research, canvas after canvas.

At times like these, art may provide its own themes of emotion, if not its subject matter; dissatisfaction with the more or less tragic expression in one canvas provides tragic intensity for the next. It was a period of despair, but teeming with accomplishment. Anguish there was, but the greater part must have been, as at other turning points in his work, perfectionism and self-criticism. Zborowski told of having visited him at this time, after having made him monthly payments for two years without receiving any pictures. He found scores of canvases stacked in a cupboard. Soutine admitted that he was in extreme need, poor health, and had not eaten for days. Zborowski hastened out to buy food. Upon his return he found Soutine in a frenzy of hysteria, endeavoring to set fire to the paintings.

One reason the Ceret paintings have gone relatively unnoticed and unliked is that they are rarely seen (Soutine did destroy a great many of them) and in black and white reproduction they are almost indecipherable. Even in a color plate the range of colors is so close and prismatic that the reduction in size defeats the eye. Each contains a wonderful mass of the colors of rather dark semi-precious stones, peridot green and jargoon brown, bloodstone and a suggestion of amethyst. Whether they are of Ceret or of some other hill-town, we cannot always be sure, but what we look for is not factual detail and positive proof of place and date, but coherency and relatedness of forms. This we do find, and thus we can keep Soutine's several sets of landscapes apart in our minds: especially those of the Oriental Pyrenees and the Maritime Alps.

One of the Ceret canvases that illustrates his experimental frame of mind is the *View of Hills* in earthy pigments with something of cubism at the center of the design and an almost abstract pattern of pyramids and diagonals. The more energetic *View of Ceret* (p. 43) deals with similar rudimentary architectural forms, but the entire agglomeration of trees and houses all tilt one way like breakers against a shore.

The Hill (p. 44) is a knotted design which makes one think of "The Book of Kells"; the trees and buildings have been completely metamorphosed and seem to twist in everlasting torment. The *Landscape, Gréolières* is still more mysterious, with a barely decipherable hill top, ascending road and tipping walls. In *Red Roofs* (p. 47) the buildings are piled above one another to make a gigantic tower which the trees threaten like boa constrictors, and the reds of the roof tiles seem to shift in the air.

Farm Girl. c.1922. Oil, 31½ x 17½″. Collection Dr. and Mrs. Harry Bakwin, New York

Woman in Pink. 1921–22. Oil, 28½″ x 21¼″. Private collection, New York

Woman in Red. c.1922. Oil, 21 x 25″. Collection Dr. and Mrs. Harry Bakwin, New York

One of the most extensive and formal of the Ceret series is the general *View of the Village* (p. 48) with a great wall of the Pyrenees darkly wooded across the center of the canvas against which roofs and pointed foothills are pitched like tents. At the right, several figures are summarily indicated in strange gesticulating attitudes.

It is important to note how little room for sky is allowed in these paintings. This may be because of the oppressiveness of the over-hanging mountains. But even when it does appear, it is painted rather like foliage, and has no real vacuity or airiness.

Certainly one of the finest of the Ceret group is the large upright *Gnarled Trees* (p. 49) with its magical fusing of autumnal reds, greens and yellows. In it there is only one of the sloping architectural patterns; the rest is hillside, bark, twig and bough, all leading upward under the houses with a wavering like flame.

Perhaps the most powerful portrait of this period is the *Man in a Green Coat* (color frontispiece), a long-nosed, inquiring-eyed man whom he painted three or four times. In this large and simple composition Soutine has eschewed almost all characterization; he has treated the form like a tree or a building in composing the curves of the arms, the slope of the chest, and the folds of the cloth; the cheek leaning against the hand like one wall on another; the other cheek in a cloud of crimson.

It was said in Montparnasse, with no denial on Soutine's part, that his first sale of a picture after coming to Paris was to Arnold Bennett, the English novelist. But the most important stroke of fortune in his life was the acquisition of his pictures by Dr. Albert C. Barnes of Philadelphia, in the winter of 1922-23. Michel George-Michel (bibl. 18) relates how Zborowski and various friends and fellow artists were alerted by Paul Guillaume to assemble a showing of virtually the entire production of the young artist, and Dr. Barnes bought a great many. Although Soutine was not enriched by this, or not for long, it made him something of a celebrity in art circles in Paris. Guillaume quotes him as expressing his astonishment: "It's incredible! All sorts of people want to lend me money." At that time Dr. Barnes wrote the first critical appraisal of Soutine in *Arts à Paris* (bibl. 2).

Free to go where he liked, his next move was to return to Cagnes, and there he turned his back on ten years of versatility and on certain potentials of his talent which he was never to attempt again. He came to detest almost all his youthful work, and the presence of so much of it in collections was a vexation to him all his life. But the importance of the work of Ceret in his career cannot be overestimated. From this point on, one has no further sense of his feeling his way or mistaking it. After 1923, he always seemed to know exactly what he sought in his art, and never seemed to doubt its value and consequence. He was no longer youthful, that is, he was only capable of development, not of change.

Soutine had been in Cagnes before, in 1918, and also during intervals of his stay at Ceret, and it is possible to misplace the origin of certain landscapes and portraits. But the most notable characteristic of Soutine's talent was his fascinated concentration on

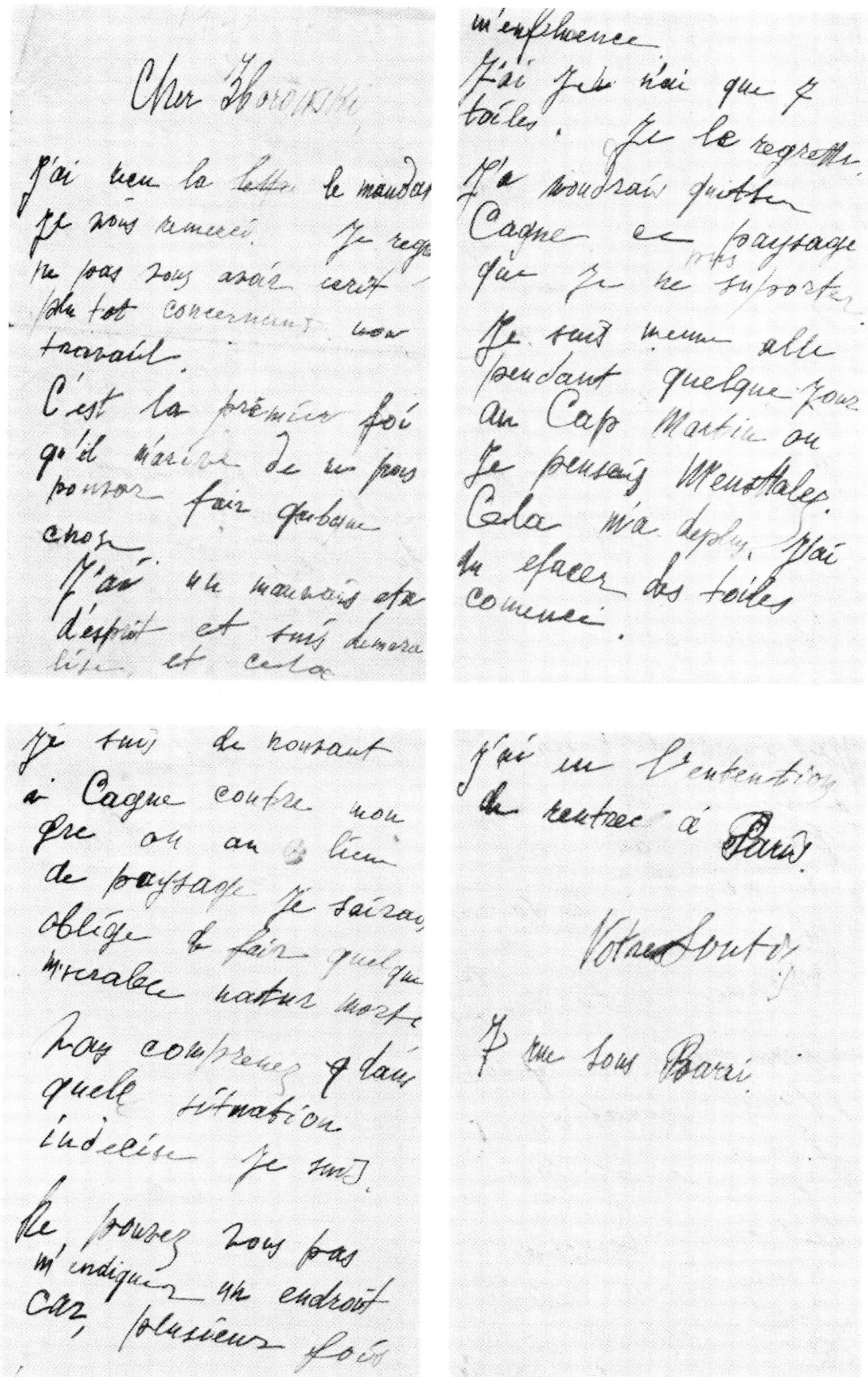

Cher Zborowski,

J'ai reçu la lettre le mandat
je vous remercie. Je regrette
de pas vous avoir écrit
plutôt concernant mon
travail.

C'est la première foi
qu'il m'arrive de ne pas
pouvoir faire quelque
chose

J'ai un mauvais état
d'esprit et suis démora
lisé, et cela

m'enfluence

J'ai je n'ai que 7
toiles. Je le regrette.
J'a voudrais quitter
Cagne ce paysage
J'ai je ne suporte très
Je suis même allé
pendant quelque jour
au Cap Martin ou
je pensais Menottales.
Cela m'a deplu. J'ai
du efacer des toiles
comencé.

Je suis de nouvant
à Cagne contre mon
gré ou au lieu
de paysage je saisais
obligé de faire quelque
mizerabe nature morte
vous comprenez dans
quelle situation
indécise je suis.

Ne pouvez vous pas
m'indiquer un endroit
car, plusieurs fois

J'ai en l'intention
de rentrer à Paris.

Votre Soutine

7 rue sous Barri

Letter from Soutine to Leopold Zborowski. 1923. Translation on page 61

Boy with Round Hat. 1922. Oil, 31½ x 24″. Private collection, New York

Portrait of the Sculptor Miestchaninoff. 1923. Oil, 32½ x 25⅝". Collection Mr. and Mrs. Oscar Miestchaninoff, New York

Landscape with Red Donkey. c.1922. Oil, 31¾ x 24½". Private collection, New York

certain forms of scenery and his acute sensibility to the light in different places. In the Pyrenees, the atmosphere is murkily warm and polychromatic, with mountains in zigzags; whereas in Cagnes it is thin, breezy, curvaceous and flowery. If we were to discover that one of his lightly animated, vivid pictures was painted in Ceret, or one of the throbbing, portentous, darkly colored ones in Cagnes, we should merely suppose that he had made one of his moves across the south of France carrying in his mind a concept of unfinished work.

His continual peregrinations were connected not only with a great physical restlessness, but with despair and apathy. Early and late in his life, his talent evidently had to lie fallow for weeks or months at a time without a stroke of work. Then all of a sudden everything would appear in his favor, his entire genius would awaken in his mind and hand, and he would produce a picture in a half-hour, in a day, or every few days, for a week or a fortnight. Year in and year out, he kept leaving Paris for the Pyrenees, the Riviera, the Beauce, Touraine, the Indres, or Lèves, leaving all those places to return to the metropolis, or moving from one province to another, as neurosis goaded him or as inspiration beckoned.

Einsild has preserved a letter to Zborowski (p. 57) written from Cagnes in 1923, which strikingly expresses his dependence on the favorable influence of a place, and his despondency when it seemed inadequate.

> *Dear Zborowski,*
>
> *I have received the money-order. I thank you. I am sorry not to have written you sooner about my work.*
>
> *It is the first time in my life that I have not been able to do anything.*
>
> *I am in a bad state of mind and I am demoralized, and that influences me.*
>
> *I have only seven canvases. I am sorry. I wanted to leave Cagnes, this landscape that I cannot endure. I even went for a few days to Cap Martin where I thought of settling down. It displeased me. I had to rub out the canvases I started.*
>
> *I am in Cagnes again, against my will, where, instead of landscapes, I shall be forced to do some miserable still lifes. You will understand in what a state of indecision I am. Can't you suggest some place for me? Because, several times I have had the intention of returning to Paris.*
>
> *Your*
>
> *Soutine*

This cry of failure immediately preceded one of the finest phases of his art. What we may call the Cagnes style is as effective in the portraits as in the scenes of tree-tops and hill towns. In the rapid, swerving portrait of the *Woman in Pink* (p. 54) leaning half out of her armchair in conversational intensity we have a disrespectful vigor not unlike the earlier portraits. But it is simpler, painted all in one set of fluent pinks, with greenish hair. The relaxed and somewhat irrational grand manner of the

Houses of Cagnes. 1923. Oil, 23⅝ x 28⅜". Collection François Reichenbach, Paris

Landscape, Cagnes. 1923–24. Oil, 21 x 25¼″. Collection M. and Mme Marcellin Castaing, Lèves, Eure-et-Loire, France

The Old Mill. c.1922. Oil, 32⅜ x 26⅛″. Collection Arthur Bradley Campbell, Palm Beach, Fla.

Woman in Red (p. 55), glancing up quizzically at an angle under her huge black hat, also stays in the mind, not as a force of nature, but as a memorable personality.

The Farm Girl (p. 53) is no less compelling in its suggestion of her immaturity and modesty, in cool tones of pink, blue and green. Perhaps the finest portrait of this period is that of his friend, the sculptor Miestchaninoff, (p. 59) which required some twenty sittings over a period of several months. An imposing man with a pout, a sidelong glance, and a vermilion nose, he sits in a fanciful chair as though it were a throne, arrayed in sky blue with snowy linen crumpled around the neck. This is magnificent painting, and here, perhaps, we can define Soutine's attitude toward a sitter whom he felt to be his equal: he conferred beauty upon him as a mark of respect; then added to it humor as an expression of his own ego.

These are speaking likenesses of more or less humble persons whom he invested with the poise of royalty, or of those who think themselves royal. Who can tell what Soutine thought of them? Surely he was enthralled by their idiosyncracy. He caricatured them, but not to amuse himself or to punish them. In the overpowering prostitutes and judges of Rouault, as in the small foxy figures of Daumier, there is satiric purpose, indignation and castigation. But there is nothing of the sort in Soutine. He has no special grievance against anyone; this is pure portraiture. He selects the salient features of these persons, their intensive gaze, outstanding ears, huge interworking hands, and renders them to excess with only summary indication of the body which he then cloaks in the magnificences of the palette. They are unforgettable.

Soon after the strong Ceret pictures, and so different in style that it is like a reversal of esthetics, comes a large view of Cagnes (color plate, p. 17) mainly in dark emerald and vibrant yellow, with a little mother-of-pearl house at the left. Once more all is tipped over sidewise but not this time as in an earthquake. The composition, held together with an armature of dark trees, is so strong that the earth stands firm under it. In spite of the brilliant sunshine, there is an effect of storm, of wind hissing and foliage whipping, and the walls of the hill town seem responsive to this, the rooftops belabored as by lightning strokes.

It is interesting to turn from this landscape to a figure picture, the *Boy with Round Hat* (p. 58). The pictorial method is very similar, with its striking darkness of garment, and almost golden pallor of the face and hands, the immense head balanced on a toy neck.

A number of the Riviera landscapes, with their cool separate colors and plenty of room allowed for the sky, suggest a sudden personal happiness, as well as a change of scene and style. In the *Landscape with Red Donkey* (p. 60) the trees not only sway and curve, but also curl upward, a little reminiscent of van Gogh's cypresses. The white stuccoed house lies back amid the branches, like a head on a pillow. In the lower left, the implausibly rubicund donkey led by a man in a white shirt seems to resound like a bell.

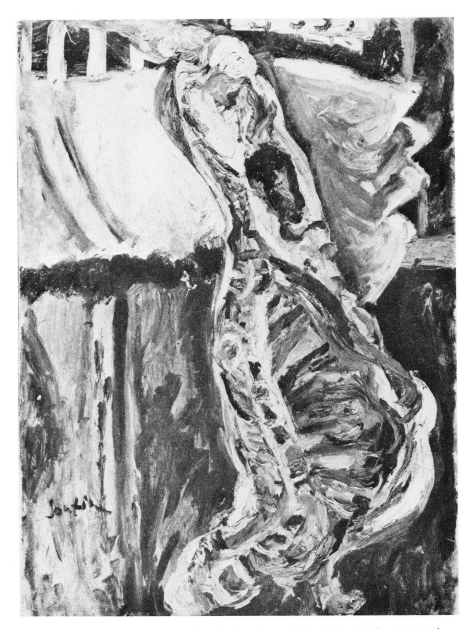

Side of Beef. 1922–23. Oil, 27½ x 20½″. Collection Mr. and Mrs. Ralph F. Colin, New York

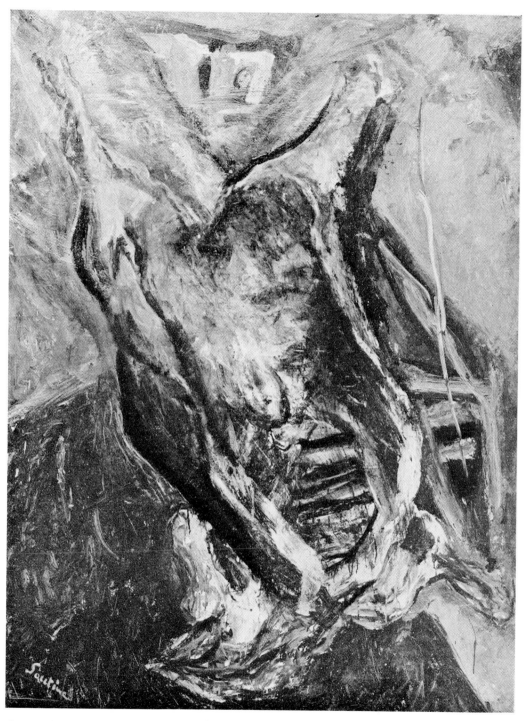

Carcass of Beef. c.1925. Oil, 55¼ x 42⅜″. The Albright Art Gallery, Buffalo, N.Y. Room of Contemporary Art

In *The Old Mill* (p. 64) — a composition which seems to fascinate him, for he used it in another picture with a different building and road — an orange yellow pours over a part of the canvas. So great was Soutine's enjoyment of his palette and his knowledge of how to multiply the shades of it by his handling of adjacent colors, that one cannot name his hues with accuracy.

In *Houses of Cagnes* (p. 62) a ribbon of road winds around the cluster of luminous houses and a yellow scarf of cloud is wafted across the hills at the top.

In several final views of Cagnes, he dispensed with almost all the darkness and dynamics and painted clusters of buildings with nothing about them but airy instability, a sort of fairy-tale quality. The finest of these is the *Landscape, Cagnes* (p. 63) in feathery evanescent tints of yellow, pink and blue. In design this is perhaps the most delicate of all Soutine's paintings.

We now come to the great series of still lifes of hulking carcasses of animals, suspended fowl, and fish. In the late twenties one scarcely heard mention of Soutine without some scandalized discourse about the gruesome circumstances of their production. When he lived in *La Ruche,* he had made friends with slaughter-house employees, and practiced painting pieces of meat which he got from them. About 1922, he painted an admirable *Side of Beef* (p. 66) in forthright realism, with the vivid red of steak, the ivory and pale gold of suet, and a finely realized hollowness inside the curved ribs.

In 1925, when he had a studio large enough in the Rue du Mont St. Gothard, he procured the entire carcass of a steer, and it was this undertaking which grew legendary. He did at least four similar canvases, three of which are now in museums: Grenoble, Amsterdam and Buffalo (p. 67) as well as sketches and smaller canvases; and meantime the steer decomposed. According to the legend, when the glorious colors of the flesh were hidden from the enthralled gaze of the painter by an accumulation of flies, he paid a wretched little model to sit beside it and fan them away. He got from the butcher a pail of blood, so that when a portion of the beef dried out, he could freshen its color. Other dwellers in the Rue du Mont St. Gothard complained of the odor of the rotting flesh, and when the police arrived Soutine harangued them on how much more important art was than sanitation or olfactory agreeableness.

These paintings are formidable, and some people never get used to them, although similar subjects by Rembrandt arouse no complaints. The Buffalo version is painted in a splendid range of scarlets, pinks and purples, with little passages of golden brightness. Upon the bulk of the creature, especially where it is convex, the color seems to flow and soak. Another magnificent steer (color plate, p. 19) is smaller and less heavy in form. It swings free on a blue ground, and pale gold predominates, while the crimson runs here and there as in blood vessels. It is not so much a dead animal as a wild phantom of the species.

After the beefs, he did a series of plucked or half-plucked fowl which preoccupied

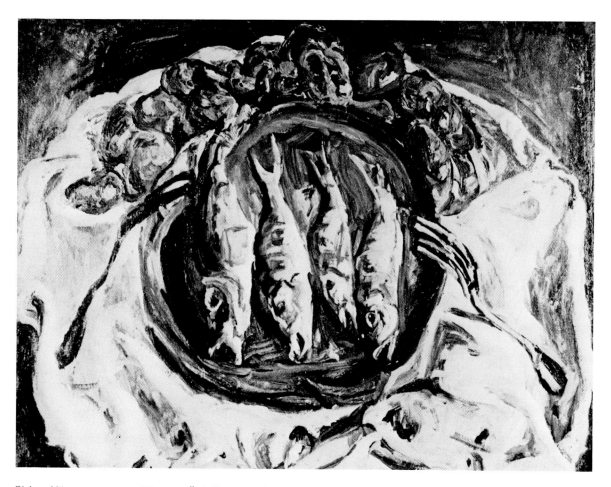

Fish and Tomatoes. c.1923. Oil, 23 x 31″. Collection Jack I. Poses, New York

Turkey. 1926. Oil, 36 x 28½″. The Museum of Modern Art, New York. Gift of Bernard Davis

Rooster. c.1926. Oil, 38⅜ x 24½". The Art Institute of Chicago. The Joseph Winterbotham Collection

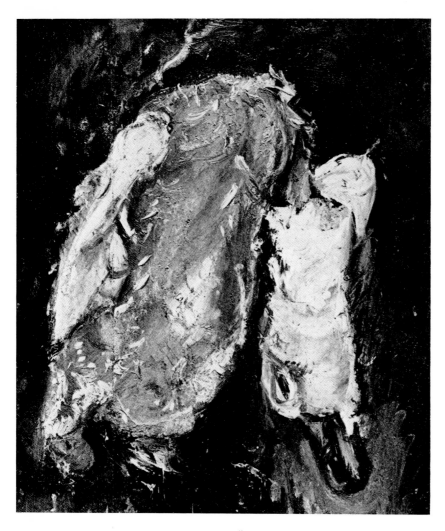

Plucked Goose. 1933. Oil on wood, 18¾ x 16¼". Collection Mrs. Lloyd Bruce Wescott, Clinton, N.J.

him over a period of two years. In the Museum of Modern Art's *Turkey* (p. 70), poised against cavernous blue, the violence of death is expressed by the gaping mouth and the agitated feathers of the neck and wings. The *Fowl with Tomatoes* (color plate, p. 15) extends the image beyond any suggestion of victimization. The greenish pallor of its skin shines out against the ruddy brick of the background; the open mouth seems to be crowing, and its feet seem to spring from the heaped tomatoes as though they were red coals. It is a bird of heraldry or poetry, not of sadism.

Zborowski told how Soutine sometimes would deliberately fast with one of his pieces of meat or poultry before him and then, with his accrued hunger, paint it. One thinks of this when one regards the grasping forks in the earlier *Fish and Tomatoes* (p. 69).

Years later he produced one more notable painting of a dead fowl, a plucked white goose (opposite), in which we may observe an abatement of the emotion having to do with subject matter and an increased concern with the purely painterly potentialities of the theme in question. This is scarcely an expressionist painting; it is more like Courbet or Manet. The bird form is now reduced to an oval, with its heavy fallen neck at the right like the handle of a pitcher. What plumage remains is rendered by white strokes over the flesh, deft feathers of pigment, so light that a breeze across the canvas might blow them away.

The skillful variability of Soutine's brush and palette are nowhere more apparent than in the two startling paintings of the ray-fish (pp. 74 and 75). The one belonging to Mr. and Mrs. Miestchaninoff is predominantly pink, of a satiny radiance and moist freshness. Mr. Reichenbach's is less subtle but rejoices in a color scheme of sharper red, turquoise and yellow. This time, the painter's bewitchment with the subject had little to do with edibility; he has depicted it like the bad dream of a child, or the villain of an animated cartoon.

Parallel to the still lifes, Soutine did a series of figure paintings of youths in the uniforms of their work or in sacerdotal garb. While the carcasses made scandal, these gave pleasure to everyone and brought him his first real prosperity.

He began with pastry cooks, probably drawn to them by his new fascination with whiteness. One of the earliest stands against a semblance of vivid red tapestry, a rather raffish creature whose baking cap in the form of a crown gives him a peculiar dignity (p. 76). Another, seated, and clutching a red handkerchief is of an even keener psychological insight, with mournful eyes, a foxy nose and prevaricative lips, like a young Figaro (p. 77).

The final pastry cook is the youngest (color plate, p. 21). He wears a turban instead of a cap, and an enveloping apron, and the face verges upon prettiness in spite of the blunt expressionist handling. Incandescent as well as irridescent, it is like some chemical fire charged with a wide range of prismatic hues.

Another masterwork of the white series is a girl, *The Communicant* (p. 78), a sharp-faced child entirely filling the canvas with her frothy finery.

At the end of the twenties there followed a group of *valets-de-chambres* in scarlet vests. One moody, with a rosy-face; another, astride a chair, seems ready to spring to his feet with necessary alacrity (pp. 80 and 81). In those years, Soutine seemed to work from color to color, the entire gamut of whites, deep blues, dusky greens, and, as always, back to his life-long color red.

The great *Page Boy at Maxim's* (p. 82) is red from head to foot. This tall, loose-jointed, bony-shouldered, homely youth, with eyes of pitch and twisted nose, with his very large out-stretched hand, is one of the supreme characters of modern art.

What a boon for Soutine that the servant class in France should have kept so many archaic styles of garment, fancy dress without frivolity, which enabled him to strike

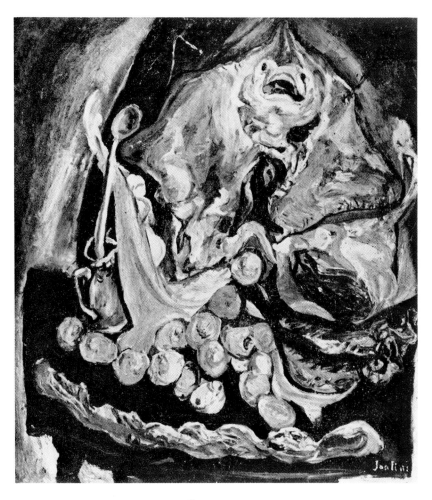

Ray-fish and Bread. c.1924. Oil, 36 x 32″. Collection François Reichenbach, Paris

that note of pitiable grandeur that was compulsive in his mind and heart, and thus avoid our modern drabness.

With his love of scarlet, it was nearly inevitable that the resplendent vestments of the church should appeal to him. In the earliest choirboy (p. 84), painted the same year as the great carcasses of beef, he played with similar overlapping reds, but refined them, and clouded them with the surplice. It is perhaps Soutine's tenderest picture. The small fervent boy stands somewhat on tip-toe as though lifted up by the music. Then followed another, half length (p. 85), rather older and notably less devout. It is one of the few personages of Soutine toward whom he seems to have taken a satirizing attitude. The last choir boy (color plate, p. 25), is seated, slightly uncomfortable but patient, holding himself tight, with elbows at his side and with clasped hands, clothed in vermilion, in a space of emerald.

74

Ray-fish. c.1924. Oil, 32 x 39½". Collection Mr. and Mrs. Oscar Miestchaninoff, New York

The summers of 1930 to 1935 Soutine spent with the Castaings at their little chateau at Lèves near Chartres. The single-minded admiration and helpfulness of this couple constitute a most important chapter of the artist's life; and thanks to their acute observation and remembrance we have a considerable knowledge of his way of working during this period. As a rule it was in frenzied exaltation and fantastic forced effort. One day, furiously at work, he dislocated his thumb and could not explain how it happened. He kept his brushes immaculate, one for each nuance of color and each magnitude of brush-stroke, beginning with about forty of them, and discarding them on the floor or the ground as fast as he used them. Three or four years after the painting of one of his views of Cagnes, Mme Castaing went there and discovered where he had established his easel for it, and was amazed to find on a stone wall little daubs of his color still bright, from the wild tossing of brushes.

The Pastry Cook. c.1922.
Oil, 60¼ x 26″. The Portland Art
Museum, Portland, Ore.

The Pastry Cook with Red Handkerchief. 1922–23. Oil, 28¾ x 21½″. Collection Mme Jean Walter, Paris

The Communicant. 1927. Oil, 31⅞ x 18⅞″. Collection Mr. and Mrs. Edward G.
Robinson, Beverly Hills, Calif.

His usual practice was to complete each picture in a single working session. From the start he knew exactly what he intended, and changed his conception scarcely at all. But on a given occasion for some reason his hand might falter, his brush miscarry. The model was restless; he suffered from his indigestion; someone's ill-considered remark stuck in his mind and vexed him. Finally he would call it a day and carry the canvas up to his room and lock it in a cupboard. Then at midnight or early next morning he would take it out and pass judgment on it, and if he found it inferior, cut it up with a knife. But this did not mean discouragement or abandonment of the picture in question. Instantly he took another canvas and began all over again. Day after day he persisted like this until he had consummated his inspiration or at least assuaged it. What he aspired to, and every so often achieved, was an effect of overwhelming excitement and uninhibited force; an instantaneous vision implacably fixed.

This was the period when he most often borrowed subject matter for his pictures from various masterpieces of the past. But the retrospective turn of his mind in middle life was altogether different from his youthful enthusiasm; it was rather culminative than formative. Soutine's taste was never eclectic, his thought about art not at all sophisticated. In his several derivative works we do not discern any intention of parody or paradox, or of a learned esthetic synthesis. Simply seized by admiration for his two or three great men, he felt a proud desire to be classified with them. Feeling his own strength, the itch of his now matured technique, he would demonstrate what he could do with the themes and problems they had proposed.

Courbet had painted an exceptionally large fish; and now likewise Soutine, modelling the eyes and mouth and gills of a salmon with bits of sharp relief, tapering it away in muted under-water colors (p. 86). Courbet had painted a large fine bull-calf in his virtuoso style, velvety white and shadowy brown; Soutine did a miniature variation upon this (p. 87) with the strongest, bluntest shorthand of his brush instead of the nineteenth-century realistic furriness.

But his most important homage to the master of Ornans was a re-creation of one of the figures in the *Demoiselles au bord de la Seine*. The search for a model was as arduous as any other phase of Soutine's creative process. Resolved upon his painting to the last detail, he would fail to find a model with the face or figure of his imagination, and despair on that account. This was the kind of problem the Castaings helped him to solve. Day after day they motored with him upon the country roads while he peered right and left, occasionally stopping for further scrutiny of someone he caught sight of. For Soutine's demoiselle in *The Siesta* (p. 89), he decided upon the wife of a railway gate-keeper, who, after the first sitting, fell into jealous suspicions and forbade her to pose again. Soutine in a terrible temper came to see them, and told the husband, "You have no right to interfere with my art. Your wife is not your property. I need her, in order to finish my picture. I must have her! I will sue you!" In due course the Castaings persuaded the gate-keeper of the respectability of Soutine's art.

The Valet. 1929. Oil, 43 x 25″. Collection Mr. and Mrs. Leigh B. Block, Chicago

The Valet. 1929.
Oil, 27¼ x 18″. Collection
Mr. and Mrs. Bernard Reis, New York

The good woman returned, the picture was recommenced.

Soutine's style bore no general relationship to Courbet's; but if one looks close, especially if one enlarges certain details, one may see what enchanted the modern painter. It was the painterliness above all, oil-painting for its own sake, with translucence and heavy texture and rugged handling. In the great recumbent figure of the gate-keeper's wife, aiming at all these effects, Soutine surpassed himself in natural energy, bold and in a sense coarse; but with marvels of lightness in the foliage and the white lace, and a fiery glow in the red blouse.

Throughout his life unquestionably Rembrandt was the painter whom Soutine most revered and to whom he did greatest honor. We have already commented on the great shocking still lifes prompted by the *Carcass of Beef* in the Louvre. Soutine, in homage to its author, made four pilgrimages to Holland. Once he sat up all night in

Page Boy at Maxim's. 1927.
Oil, 60⅜ x 26″. The Albright Art
Gallery, Buffalo, N.Y.
Room of Contemporary Art

a third-class compartment to Amsterdam, went straight from the railway station to the Rijks Museum, and sat all day long on the bench facing *The Jewish Bride* until every inch of it was indelible in his mind; and when the museum closed, took the train again, all night long back to Paris, to his studio and whatever work he had in progress. No canvas of his seems to have been directly inspired by that treasure of the Rijks Museum; but in about 1927 he began to be haunted by the *Woman Bathing* in the National Gallery in London, and derived from it one of his most powerful and affecting canvases (p. 91).

This necessitated another model hunt; days of excitement and wearisome research around the countryside until he found a satisfactory peasant woman working in a field. At first she was suspicious of immorality, then fearful of madness, but at last was persuaded to stand in a brook in one corner of the Castaing property, in the shadow of a masonry arch; and the usual sequence of days of Soutine's creative distress and ecstasy followed.

On one of those days clouds suddenly gathered overhead, and it began to rain. The peasant woman cried out to him to stop and let her take shelter somewhere. He shouted orders back at her, not to move an inch or she would be to blame for ruining his work. The rain fell, the thunder rolled, and it was dark, but Soutine went on working by the light of imagination. At last he came to his senses and was surprised to find himself drenched to the skin, and the model in hysterical tears, shaking with cold and fright.

The picture preserved in the end is one of Soutine's unquestionable masterworks; one in which he extended his imagination, putting himself, if not in his subject's place, much nearer so than was his wont. It is a work of sincere sympathy, strange empathy. As he looked at that poor woman — having more or less forced her, that is, bullied and cajoled and purchased her, to come and be looked at — he seemed appreciative above all of the offense to her modesty, the posture of her embarrassment and shame. It is far from the pleasurable, amorous feeling of the Rembrandt which inspired it; it expresses rather the vague generalized sense of guilt of every man toward every woman.

There is only one nude by Soutine (p. 92), so far as we know, a small but important sketch, like a footnote to the foregoing great canvas. This surely was no country-woman; probably a model, certainly not self-conscious, accustomed to the regard of men, artistic or otherwise. She has just stepped forward out of the dark of corridor or doorway, into an unflattering light; her exceptionally large eyes glitter at us. In a way it is a humorous picture, as some of Rembrandt's are; a more or less professional Susanna, with no elders visible.

As already specified with reference to Courbet, these canvases of the early thirties are scarcely to be scrutinized for influences upon Soutine's technique and style. In the main his indebtedness was only for an idea or a pose; an appeal to imagination.

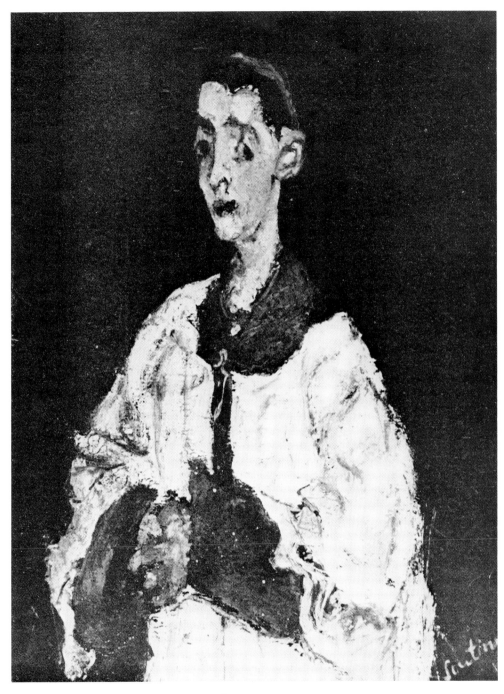

Choir Boy with Surplice. c.1928. Oil, 25 x 19¾". Collection Mme Jean Walter, Paris

Opposite: *Choir Boy*. 1925. Oil, 38¾ x 21¼". Collection M. and Mme Marcellin Castaing, Lèves, Eure-et-Loire, France

Salmon. 1933. Oil on wood, 13¾ x 30½″. Collection Mr. and Mrs. Ralph F. Colin, New York

Nevertheless, a comparison with Rembrandt, not just as to these figures of women but in general, in a considerable part of his mature production, offers one or two points of esthetic interest. Single-figured central composition, so frequent in the work of the great Dutchman, was Soutine's almost constant practice; the simplest possible arrangement, like a piece of sculpture in a niche. This is not to be observed only in the indoor pictures; someone framed as in a window or archway or entrance way, something laid out as in a vitrine. He would sometimes similarly enshrine a building or a tree (or group of trees as a unit); in which case some narrowed pointed village-perspective, or unrealistic sky drawn down close, was made to serve as a niche. Rembrandt played games with light, blotting it out here, bringing it in sideways there. Not content with just dramatizing his model by means of it, he made a drama of chiaroscuro itself. Soutine shows no such concern for optical realities. As a rule he is just visually romancing in this respect, not trying to give plausibility to any object or situation. His background is not shadow; it is blueness, greenness, or brownness. No sun, lamp or fire ever cast this or that marvelous beam or glow — his rich palette and forty brushes cast it.

What painting could be more luminous in this unrealistic way than the little *House at Oisème* (p. 93) curiously yellowish, lit up by something more than daylight, it might be refraction from gold. It is an ancient house settling into the earth, in a nest of trees, under two inexplicable small clouds like smoke going up.

A no less important work, *Chartres Cathedral* (color plate, p. 27) seems to have been

The Little Calf. 1934. Oil on wood, 16¼ x 20". Collection M. and Mme Marcellin Castaing, Lèves, Eure-et-Loire, France

intended as a piece of mysticism, glorifying and rejoicing, yet solemn. It is in jewel-colors, but not this time the famous intense shades suggestive of passion and sacrifice; an extraordinary range of delicate tints instead, an opalescence — greenish-blue of sea-water, gray of sea-water, and a bit of vivid rosiness like quartz. It seems a tribute of one art to the other, the contemporary easel-painter gladly sacrificing some of his individualism to the great work of the collective medieval architects; its intricacies of structure, minutiae of carved stone and inset glass, all simply and fervently rendered.

Twice during the painting of this picture Soutine enlarged it by roughly nailing new strips of wood to the original panel so that it had to go immediately to an expert restorer. Soutine never seemed at all embarrassed about putting his purchasers to this extra trouble and expense. It was a shortcoming of his talent, not knowing how to foresee the proportions of his subject matter within the dimensions of his board or canvas; there were often superfluities or insufficiencies.

Courbet: Study for
Les Demoiselles aux bords de la Seine.
Private collection, Paris

For many years he preferred to paint over old pictures, as providing a more gratifying or effective surface to his brush. Every so often he would make an excursion to the Paris flea-market and bring back a great bundle of cheap, unprepossessing pictures. The writer once saw a landscape half-painted, over a nineteenth-century bouquet of firecracker-red flowers; it was astonishing that Soutine could have worked against the visual shock and interference. His eye not only discerned infinitesimally the variations of his chosen colors, but seemed to screen out every sort of irrelevance.

It has been estimated that we have left only one out of ten of his canvases. For the most part this refers to that destructiveness in the course of creation which has been mentioned. But he came to detest almost his entire production prior to 1923, resenting the fact that so much of it remained in great collections; and whenever possible he took delight in acquiring early pictures for the express purpose of demolishing them. Also, when he rejected unsatisfactory versions of work in progress, he sometimes did not entirely destroy the bits and pieces. Unscrupulous persons would get hold of them, have them recanvased and retouched, and offer them for sale; hence a number of so-called false Soutines. Upon one occasion an inferior picture was acquired by a distinguished but unfamiliar collector who wanted Soutine to sign it. Soutine courteously went to see him. Upon entering the room where it hung, he turned pale, muttered incomprehensively, fumbled in his pockets for a jack-knife, slashed the picture irremediably and rushed away. At a time when his work was in great demand, with several important collectors waiting their turn to purchase from him, a shrewd

The Siesta. 1934. Oil, 28¼ x 35¾". Collection M. and Mme Marcellin Castaing, Lèves, Eure-et-Loire, France

Rembrandt: *Woman Bathing*.
National Gallery, London

young man bought and showed to Soutine a dubious canvas, certain to offend him, and was given a small authentic picture in exchange.

In the early thirties, Soutine was at the peak of his career. From that point on he was entitled to all the fortune and world-wide repute that art can confer, if only he had continued to paint as diligently as in the previous decade. He had resolved and alleviated his preoccupation with painful subject matter. He had transcended all the classifications of the schools, expressionism, neo-classicism, and so forth; on the other hand his art no longer seemed very eccentric to anyone. But by his nature Soutine could not be contented or easy in his mind; and in the final decade one may observe certain changes in his painting technique, with perhaps a new orientation of his enthusiasms about painters of the past. He did not live to bring all this to fruition in any great number of canvases, but his purpose was manifested plainly enough; to become somewhat less dependent upon his genius for color, to achieve a stronger mastery of his third dimension and of linear design.

It is easy to see the gradual development of this tendency if we look first at characteristic works of the late twenties, then at his subsequent production in more or less the same category; for example, portraiture. In the *Portrait of Boy in Blue* (color plate, p. 23), a powerful, true portrait, a speaking likeness, the method of portrayal is by accumulation of tiny patches of color, one impinging on the other, close in value,

Woman Wading. 1931. Oil, 44½ x 28½″. Collection M. and Mme Marcellin Castaing, Lèves, Eure-et-Loire, France

Female Nude. c.1933.
Oil, 18⅛ x 10⅝″. Collection
Mr. and Mrs. Ralph F. Colin, New York

seeming to fuse or melt together. There are no very marked contrasts except between the two main areas, flesh and fabric. Only some outside contours have been emphasized by deepening the recessive shadow, somewhat as Cézanne did.

Similarly, in the *Portrait of Maria Lani* (p. 94), the lightness of the actress' face against the profound blue background is composed of soft touches without particular dimension or direction. Only the eyes and high eyebrows and clever lips are drawn in on the surface. The *Portrait of Madeleine Castaing* (p. 95) brooding in expression and attitude, dressed in crimson and in an enveloping dark cloak, also is a kind of construction in masses, a sculpturing of colors. Even the head of *The Polish Girl*

House at Oisème. 1934. Oil on wood, 27 x 26″. Collection Richards H. Emerson, New York

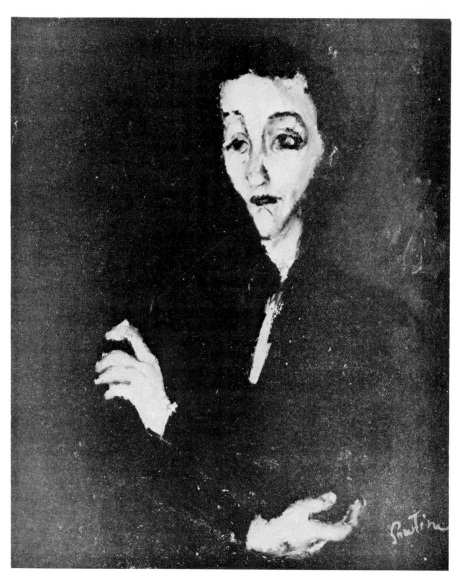

Portrait of Maria Lam. 1929. Oil, 28¼ x 23¼". Collection Mr. and Mrs. Sam A. Lewisohn, New York

Portrait of Madeleine Castaing. c.1928. Oil, 39⅜ x 28⅞″. The Museum of Modern Art, New York. Extended loan from Miss Adelaide Milton de Groot

The Polish Girl. 1926.
Oil, 20 x 18″. Collection
Mrs. H. Harris Jonas, New York

(above), which is sketchy in a sense, that is, lyrical — an expression of the mood and animation of the sitter rather than the reality of flesh and bony structure — seems the slowest kind of sketching; cumulative caressing touches, flesh-pinkness and red-headedness.

All this was work of the twenties. Now, early in the thirties, observe the very different handling, not in entire pictures to begin with, but here and there, in details of some we have already examined: the almost chiselled or hammered little rectangle of the body of *The Little Calf;* the broad treatment of the forehead and nose of the last of the choir boys, characterizing the face with a single directed gleam, and the quick red mimicry of the red cloth in some places. Note how Soutine here has loaded his brush with light hues and unloaded them on top of more shadowy passages; and how he has elongated his stroke and taken shortcuts with it, as though with a heavy pen or blunt crayon.

In the *Servant Girl in Blue* (opposite) the change is complete, it amounts to innovation, though it concerns only the manipulation of the pigments — the composition is still niche-like. Cerulean and rosy, the colors seem less rich but more instant, more

Servant Girl in Blue. 1934–35. Oil, 20¼ x 20⅝". Kunstmuseum, Lucerne, Switzerland

Portrait of a Young Man. 1935. Oil, 22 x 13¼". Collection Dr. and Mrs. Harry Bakwin, New York

Woman in Profile. 1937. Oil, 18½ x 11″. The Phillips Gallery, Washington, D.C.

immediate, than ever before; running somehow more obediently from the brush on to the canvas to establish the buxom youthful form inside the clean blue cloth with almost beribboning highlights, in an easy peaceable atmosphere.

In the small *Portrait of a Young Man* (p. 98), exquisite mocking likeness of an over-formal little personage, the face and hands are all composed of these tiny ribbons of fleshcolor. *The Concierge* (opposite) shows facile application of a singular lightness over duskiness, and strong filling in of the coils of the hair and strong spotting of the pupils of the eye, as with ink. The result is a verisimilitude so quick and lively that one is reminded of Franz Hals, even of certain of Hals' late nineteenth-century followers. In the *Woman in Profile* (p. 99), there is an extreme spirituality; an acute scrutinizing or questioning position of the head, a pouting thoughtfulness, which makes it one of Soutine's finest portraits; with something of the quasi-caricatural aspect of the portraits of the period of Cagnes, for example, the *Woman in Pink*, but so effortless now, and for Soutine, singularly respectful and pleasant.

Perhaps by that time Soutine was tired or ill. He did very little of this simple and pleasing work. In some way the change of his manner of painting was not benign or not lucky. It may indeed have seemed less open to the charge of clumsiness, formlessness, but possibly to some slight extent he had fallen into formula. Mastery meant easiness, and after life having been so difficult, and the pursuit of art so daemonic, perhaps his facility failed to interest him when he had it. It was no mere matter of his being spoiled by success. Never in his elder years was he as prosperous as in the brief period of the pastry cooks and the choir boys, simply because he never painted enough. The number of his working hours, per month or per year, diminished. There were not canvases enough to occupy the dealers, or to stimulate new collectors. Most surprisingly and lamentably, his choices of subjects to paint sometimes seemed idle or thoughtless. A kind of lack of emotion, listlessness, colorlessness, developed in some paintings and detracted from entire admiration. In all this one feels somewhat borne out in the suggestion that the intensest factor in Soutine's art, the secret of his particular expressionism, may have been only *how* to express, not what — his ghastly anxiety lest the power and skill of his brush fail to fulfill the vision in his mind's eye. In the increase of facility, his zeal to work diminished; brilliance of style took away some of his incentive.

The last of Soutine's pictures in an important set or series were landscapes featuring trees. Tree worship is a cult anciently established in the Lithuanian part of Russia. In Soutine's youth there were still arboreal rites in villages not far removed from Smilovitchi, and at the foot of any very noble specimen in the countryside one might find offerings. One can only conjecture whether he had this in mind years later. In any case no other notable contemporary painter has offered us portraiture of so many individual trees of distinct character, with strong romantic implications.

One of his greatest is the central ornament of the village of Vence, beyond Cagnes,

The Concierge. c.1935.
Oil, 12 x 10¾". Collection
Paul Gardner, Kansas City, Mo.

vast, circled round with a green bench, against a vista of small shops. In the one version, called *Small Town Square, Vence* (p. 102), the trunk and the branches are stiff and angular, like a strange wishbone; and the entire scene, on earth and in the sky, is sunshiny, the vivid, dazzling, nervous south. In another (p. 103), the trunk is extremely heavy and curvaceous, and the small boughs lie one over the other in loose circles forming a kind of mesh in which shadow lies and is slowly stirred by breeze. Effects like this, a rendering of the air itself in motion, not the blue of the sky but light itself, supreme whiteness fragmented by the leaves, were sought by Soutine again and again until the end of his life. In the Vence pictures the principal charm is a magical whiteness of the walls gleaming under and through the trees; the radiance leading the eye along sideways to a small and abruptly recessive street, fantastically bright-colored, like a kaleidoscope held still.

The *Alley of Trees* (color plate, p. 29) was painted at the Grand Prés near Chartres; it was a theme which he undertook several times, always effectively. Painted in extraordinarily thick impasto, as years before in Ceret, apparently they are poplar trees, growing in the collective shape of a very tall arch or portal, on which the upper-most twigs and the brightness of the sky seem to ramble in delicate liveliness. The

Small Town Square, Vence. 1929. Oil, 28 x 18¼". The Art Institute of Chicago. The Joseph Winterbotham Collection

Tree of Vence. 1929. Oil, 32 x 24¼". Collection Mrs. Lloyd Bruce Wescott, Clinton, N.J.

Windy Day, Auxerre. 1939. Oil, 19¼ x 28⅝″. The Phillips Gallery, Washington, D.C.

light gleams through the boughs, a mysterious little crimson cottage shines out from beyond the tree trunks, and two miniature personages somewhat grandly gesture as they proceed along the narrow road.

In another almost entirely green landscape painted some years later (p. 109), there is a bank of many trees with slender trunks all bent in the same direction, reflected in a pool, and on the bank someone is sleeping. It has an impersonal grandeur, detached from every sort of pride and distress of ordinary mortals.

In one of the very last canvases, *Autumn Trees, Champigny* (p. 110), the design is more complex; all the trees in the center, pruned high up on the trunk, have the form of a large harp with heavy strings; and a different species of trees curves away at one side in the form of a wing; and the foreground is suggestive of the form of a cockle-shell. Again the light, divided and subdivided by vegetation, gleams white as linen, blue as flax. The flutings of the cockle-shell represent ruts of a road, and a woman and child depart on it. Surely this humble, nevertheless mystic route does honor to Hobbema and other baroque masters; perhaps also to Chaplin, for the humorous and lonely departures at the conclusion of certain films.

Seated Child in Blue. 1936. Oil, 13 x 9½". Collection M. and Mme Marcellin Castaing, Lèves, Eure-et-Loire, France

Andrée Collie, the novelist, who knew Soutine late in his life, published the year after his death an excellent brief reminiscence of his character (bibl. 7). Though she viewed him severely, her pages evoke his personality perhaps better than any other text. It was a period when he was working very little, idling in cafés with flattering chance acquaintances, or shutting himself up in a darkly curtained, stuffy hotel bedroom, trying to improve his mind by reading philosophy, and falling asleep to pass the time.

One day she said to him, "You have had great unhappiness in your life, haven't

Return from School after the Storm. 1939. Oil, 17 x 19½″. The Phillips Gallery, Washington, D.C.

you, Soutine?" He gave her a look of surprise, and shaking her by the arm, answered, "No! What makes you think that? I have always been a happy man." And his worn face lit up with pride and joy.

She recalled his reading the editorials of Maurras in *l'Action Française,* with some admiration, and explained that he was a believer in social inequality "because it presented magnificent opportunities for everyone." It seemed to him that luck was a more uplifting and fortifying concept for men's minds than mere justice. When one of his painter-friends failed miserably he expressed compassion for him, but then added, "What I don't understand is why he goes on painting. I would have stopped it had I not succeeded. I might have become a boxer. . . ."

During the war, in 1940, Soutine was staying with his friend Einsild, at Civry. He

106

Girl in Polka Dot Dress. 1942.
Oil, 30¼ x 20⅛″. Collection
Jacques Guérin, Paris

was painting landscapes. The curé of a nearby village was curious about his painting, and watched him whenever he could. Soutine had a horror of this, and would hide his canvases. The curé, angry and suspicious, went to the police and denounced Soutine as a foreign agent. He was arrested, and kept in jail for three days.

A little later, when Civry was occupied, a German officer engaged him in conversation in the street. Upon learning that Soutine was an artist, he asked him to paint his four-year-old son from a photograph. Soutine dared not refuse the request, and promptly provided a most conventional and painstaking miniature. With what we know of his intransigeance, this may be taken as a revelation of his tragic, submissive state of mind about the Germans.

In the late twenties, there hung in the Rue la Boetie a small painting by Courbet

Maternity. 1942. Oil, 25½ x 20″. Collection M. and Mme Marcellin Castaing, Lèves, Eure-et-Loire, France

Landscape with Reclining Figure. 1942. Oil, 28¼ x 35½″. Collection Jacques Guérin, Paris

of two children on the beach at St. Aubain. Soutine admired it and in tyrannous enthusiasm took all his friends to see it. It represented a man and woman resting in the background on a green cliff and two little children standing alone on their joint shadow on the sand, gazing straight ahead. The picture was brought to America, and Soutine could not have seen it after 1930. But in the war years, those children still haunted his mind. Is it not they, at a distance upon the road in *Windy Day, Auxerre* (p. 104), dwarfed by tormented trees, and running in *Return from School After the Storm* (p. 106)? Perhaps in that twilight of his life, in that eclipse in the life of his adopted country, children two by two in brotherhood or friendship may have seemed to him an image of the condition of all human beings on earth, more acceptable than any other ideal furnished to his mind by patriotism, or religion, or romantic love.

There are other late representations of children, very different from these apparitional couples blown along vague roads. In a picture of two boys resting upon a log,

Autumn Trees, Champigny. 1942. Oil, 30¾ x 23¼″. Collection M. and Mme Marcellin Castaing, Lèves, Eure-et-Loire, France

the atmosphere is sinister, implying something about the unhappiness of youngsters left to their own devices. There is a miniature portrait of an infant seated alone in what appears to be a nursery bedroom, happy and dreamy, sucking its finger-tips; a masterpiece of abbreviation in Soutine's largest-scale virtuoso brushwork, on a very tiny canvas (p. 105). In *Girl in Polka Dot Dress* (p. 107), a mysterious figure of a little girl leans upon a gate or fence, and in the distance a row of tree-trunks makes one think of prison bars.

In another late painting, *Maternity* (p. 108), all his greatness spoke out, and in a new way. In this great work, his sentiment about children gives way to a profound epigrammatic utterance. The mother is the noblest of his women, with no class-consciousness now, no perversity, nor even excess of pity, or unkind scrutiny. The child lies back in her lap, in defeat or exhaustion, as though on a field of battle, his garb a kind of uniform. This is no mere child; it is every man, and all men are children. It reminds one of the Mayan Goddess of War in the Peabody Museum in Boston which Soutine may never have known — a little figure looking down with pitying countenance upon warriors lying in her lap.

Soutine suffered no specific persecution or violence during the war. In 1940, he was offered an opportunity to come to America, but he would not take advantage of it. He lived with a friend at Champigny-sur-Veuldre, in Touraine. Having suffered from stomach ulcers for half his life, the war surely aggravated his nervous state, with a gradual, fatal effect upon his health. One day in the summer of 1943, he was terribly stricken. His friend took him in a car to the nearest hospital where an immediate operation was advised. For some reason they decided against it, and drove on two hundred kilometres to Paris. By the time they reached the clinic of Dr. Ollivier, Soutine was in a desperate condition. The operation performed by Professor Gosset was unsuccessful, and Soutine died a few hours later, on August 9, 1943. He was buried in Montparnasse Cemetery.

CATALOG OF THE EXHIBITION

Exhibition dates: New York, October 31, 1950 to January 7, 1951; Cleveland, January 30 to March 18, 1951.

An asterisk (*) preceding the catalog entry indicates that the painting is illustrated. In listing the dimensions, height precedes width.

**The Artist's Studio, Cité Falguière.* 1915. Oil on canvas, 25½ x 19½". Private collection, New York. *Ill. p. 32*

**Still Life with Soup Tureen.* c.1916. Oil on canvas, 24 x 29". Lent by Mr. and Mrs. Ralph F. Colin, New York. *Ill. p. 36*

**Still Life with Chair.* 1916–17. Oil on canvas, 29 x 21½". Lent by Dr. Harry Austin Blutman, New York. *Ill. p. 37*

The Spotted Vase. c.1917. Oil on canvas, 25⅝ x 18". Lent by Mr. and Mrs. Oscar Miestchaninoff, New York

**Self Portrait.* c.1917. Oil on canvas, 18 x 21½". Lent by Henry Pearlman, New York. *Ill. p. 34*

**Reclining Woman.* 1917. Oil on canvas, 23¼ x 36½". Private collection, New York. *Ill. p. 40*

**Still Life with Fish.* c.1917. Oil on canvas, 16 x 25". Lent by Miss Adelaide Milton de Groot, New York. *Ill. p. 38*

**Still Life with Pheasant.* c.1918. Oil on canvas, 35½ x 23". Lent by Frederic R. Mann, Philadelphia, Pa. *Ill. p. 39*

Brace of Pheasants. c.1919. Oil on canvas, 25⅞ x 19⅞". Lent by Leonard C. Hanna, Jr., Cleveland, Ohio

**Red Gladioli.* c.1919. Oil on canvas, 21½ x 18". Lent by Mr. and Mrs. Harry Lewis Winston, Birmingham, Mich. *Ill. in color p. 13*

**View of Montmartre.* c.1919. Oil on canvas, 25¾ x 32". Lent by William E. Campbell, Mobile, Ala. *Ill. p. 41*

**Landscape with Church Tower.* c.1919. Oil on canvas, 21⅛ x 28¾". Lent by Henry Pearlman, New York. *Ill. p. 42*

Landscape, Ceret. c.1919. Oil on canvas, 21¼ x 25¾". Lent by Mr. and Mrs. Oscar Miestchaninoff, New York

**View of Ceret.* c.1919. Oil on canvas, 21¼ x 28¾". Kunstmuseum, Lucerne, Switzerland. *Ill. p. 43*

**The Hill.* c.1919. Oil on canvas, 29 x 21¾". Lent by Mr. and Mrs. Sidney Janis, New York. *Ill. p. 44*

Landscape, Gréolières. c.1920. Oil on canvas, 31⅝ x 23⅝". Lent by Mr. and Mrs. Clifford Odets, New York.

**Village Square.* c.1920. Oil on canvas, 29⅞ x 33¾". Lent by Henry Pearlman, New York. *Ill. p. 45*

**Red Roofs.* c.1920. Oil on canvas, 32 x 25½". Lent by Henry Pearlman, New York. *Ill. p. 47*

**Gnarled Trees.* c.1921. Oil on canvas, 28¾ x 36¼". Lent by Mr. and Mrs. Ralph F. Colin, New York. *Ill. p. 49*

**Man in a Green Coat.* c.1921. Oil on canvas, 34⅞ x 21¾". Lent by Mr. and Mrs. Samuel A. Marx, Chicago. *Frontispiece*

**View of the Village.* c.1921. Oil on canvas, 28¾ x 38". Private collection, New York. *Ill. p. 48*

**The Haunted House, Ceret.* 1921–22. Oil on canvas, 31 x 34". Lent by Dr. Harry Austin Blutman, New York. *Ill. p. 51*

**Woman in Pink.* 1921–22. Oil on canvas, 28½ x 21¼". Private collection, New York. *Ill. p. 54*

**Woman in Red.* c.1922. Oil on canvas, 21 x 25". Lent by Dr. and Mrs. Harry Bakwin, New York. *Ill. p. 55*

**Farm Girl.* c.1922. Oil on canvas, 31½ x 17½". Lent by Dr. and Mrs. Harry Bakwin, New York. *Ill. p. 53*

**Landscape with Red Donkey.* c.1922. Oil on canvas, 31¾ x 24½". Private collection, New York. *Ill. p. 60*

**Landscape at Cagnes.* c.1922. Oil on canvas, 28½ x 36½". Lent by Mr. and Mrs. Ralph F. Colin, New York. *Ill. in color p. 17*

**Boy with Round Hat.* 1922. Oil on canvas, 31½ x 24" Private collection, New York. *Ill. p. 58*

**The Old Mill.* c.1922. Oil on canvas, 32⅜ x 26⅛". Lent by Arthur Bradley Campbell, Palm Beach, Fla. *Ill. p. 64*

**The Pastry Cook.* c.1922. Oil on canvas, 60¼ x 26". The Portland Art Museum, Portland, Ore. *Ill. p. 76*

**The Pastry Cook with Red Handkerchief.* 1922–23. Oil on canvas, 28¾ x 21½". Lent by Mme Jean Walter, Paris. *Ill. p. 77*

**Side of Beef.* 1922–23. Oil on canvas, 27½ x 20½". Lent by Mr. and Mrs. Ralph F. Colin, New York. *Ill. p. 66*

Landscape. c.1923. Oil on canvas, 31⅞ x 26¼". Lent by Henri Matisse, Paris

Fish and Tomatoes. c.1923. Oil on canvas, 23 x 31". Lent by Jack I. Poses, New York. *Ill. p. 69*

House of Cagnes. 1923. Oil on canvas, 23⅝ x 28⅜". Lent by François Reichenbach, Paris. *Ill. p. 62*

Portrait of the Sculptor Miestchaninoff. 1923. Oil on canvas, 32½ x 25⅝". Lent by Mr. and Mrs. Oscar Miestchaninoff, New York. *Ill. p. 59*

Landscape, Cagnes. 1923–24. Oil on canvas, 21 x 25¼". Lent by M. and Mme Marcellin Castaing, Lèves, Eure-et-Loire, France. *Ill. p. 63*

Ray-fish. c.1924. Oil on canvas, 32 x 39½". Lent by Mr. and Mrs. Oscar Miestchaninoff, New York. *Ill. p. 75*

Calf with Red Curtain. c.1924. Oil on canvas, 31¾ x 19¼". Private collection, New York

Ray-fish and Bread. c.1924. Oil on canvas, 36 x 32". Lent by François Reichenbach, Paris. *Ill. p. 74*

Carcass of Beef. c.1925. Oil on canvas, 55¼ x 42⅜". The Albright Art Gallery, Buffalo, N.Y. Room of Contemporary Art. *Ill. p. 67*

Boy in Black. c.1925. Oil on canvas, 18⅜ x 12⅝". Lent by Dr. and Mrs. Harry Bakwin, New York

Choir Boy. 1925. Oil on canvas, 38¾ x 21¼". Lent by M. and Mme Marcellin Castaing, Lèves, Eure-et-Loire, France. *Ill. p. 84*

Fowl with Tomatoes. 1925–26. Oil on canvas, 39½ x 17¾". Lent by Bernard Reichenbach, Paris. *Ill. in color p. 15*

The Polish Girl. 1926. Oil on canvas, 20 x 18". Lent by Mrs. H. Harris Jonas, New York. *Ill. p. 96*

Turkey. 1926. Oil on canvas, 36 x 28½". The Museum of Modern Art, New York. Gift of Bernard Davis. *Ill. p. 70*

Rooster. c.1926. Oil on canvas, 38⅜ x 24½". The Art Institute of Chicago. The Joseph Winterbotham Collection. *Ill. p. 71*

Carcass of Beef. 1926. Oil on canvas, 45¾ x 31⅞". Lent by Mme Germaine Bignou, Paris. *Ill. in color p. 19*

The Pastry Cook. c.1927. Oil on canvas, 30⅛ x 27¼". Lent by Mr. and Mrs. Lee A. Ault, New York. *Ill. in color p. 21*

The Communicant. 1927. Oil on canvas, 31⅞ x 18⅞". Lent by Mr. and Mrs. Edward G. Robinson, Beverly Hills, California. *Ill. p. 78*

Page Boy at Maxim's. 1927. Oil on canvas, 60⅜ x 26". The Albright Art Gallery, Buffalo, N.Y. Room of Contemporary Art. *Ill. p. 82*

Portrait of Madeleine Castaing. c.1928. Oil on canvas, 39⅜ x 28⅞". The Museum of Modern Art, New York. Extended loan from Miss Adelaide Milton de Groot. *Ill. p. 95*

Girl in Red. c.1928. Oil on canvas, 31⅞ x 23⅝". Lent by Mr. and Mrs. Albert D. Lasker, New York

Choir Boy with Surplice. c.1928. Oil on canvas, 25 x 19¾". Lent by Mme Jean Walter, Paris. *Ill. p. 85*

The Valet. 1929. Oil on canvas, 27¼ x 18". Lent by Mr. and Mrs. Bernard Reis, New York. *Ill. p. 81*

The Valet. 1929. Oil on canvas, 43 x 25". Lent by Mr. and Mrs. Leigh B. Block, Chicago. *Ill. p. 80*

Portrait of Maria Lani. 1929. Oil on canvas, 28¼ x 23¼". Lent by Mr. and Mrs. Sam A. Lewisohn, New York. *Ill. p. 94*

Portrait of Boy in Blue. 1929. Oil on canvas, 30 x 23". Lent by Mr. and Mrs. Ralph F. Colin, property of Ralph F. Colin, Jr., New York. *Ill. in color p. 23*

Small Town Square, Vence. 1929. Oil on canvas, 28 x 18¼". The Art Institute of Chicago. The Joseph Winterbotham Collection. *Ill. p. 102*

Tree of Vence. 1929. Oil on canvas, 32 x 24¼". Lent by Mrs. Lloyd Bruce Wescott, Clinton, N.J. *Ill. p. 103*

Seated Choir Boy. c.1930. Oil on wood, 25¼ x 14¼". Private collection, Paris. *Ill. in color p. 25*

Woman Wading. 1931. Oil on canvas, 44½ x 28½". Lent by M. and Mme Marcellin Castaing, Lèves, Eure-et-Loire, France. *Ill. p. 91*

Female Nude. c.1933. Oil on canvas, 18⅛ x 10⅝". Lent by Mr. and Mrs. Ralph F. Colin, New York. *Ill. p. 92*

Salmon. 1933. Oil on wood, 13¾ x 30½". Lent by Mr. and Mrs. Ralph F. Colin, New York. *Ill. p. 86*

Plucked Goose. 1933. Oil on wood, 18¾ x 16¼". Lent by Mrs. Lloyd Bruce Wescott, Clinton, N.J. *Ill. p. 72*

Chartres Cathedral. 1933. Oil on wood, 36 x 19½". Lent by Mrs. Lloyd Bruce Wescott, Clinton, N.J. *Ill. in color, p. 27*

The Siesta. 1934. Oil on canvas, 28¼ x 35¾". Lent by M. and Mme Marcellin Castaing, Lèves, Eure-et-Loire, France. *Ill. p. 89*

House at Oisème. 1934. Oil on wood, 27 x 26". Lent by Richards H. Emerson, New York. *Ill. p. 93*

The Little Calf. 1934. Oil on wood, 16¼ x 20". Lent by M. and Mme Marcellin Castaing, Lèves, Eure-et-Loire, France. *Ill. p. 87*

Servant Girl in Blue. 1934–35. Oil on canvas, 20¼ x 20⅝". Kunstmuseum, Lucerne, Switzerland. *Ill. p. 97*

Portrait of a Young Man. 1935. Oil on canvas, 22 x 13¼". Lent by Dr. and Mrs. Harry Bakwin, New York. *Ill. p. 98*

The Concierge. c.1935. Oil on canvas, 12 x 10¾". Lent by Paul Gardner, Kansas City, Mo. *Ill. p. 101*

Seated Child in Blue. 1936. Oil on canvas, 13 x 9½". Lent by M. and Mme Marcellin Castaing, Lèves, Eure-et-Loire, France. *Ill. p. 105*

Alley of Trees. 1936. Oil on canvas, 30 x 27¼". Lent by Mr. and Mrs. Ralph F. Colin, property of Miss Pamela T. Colin, New York. *Ill. in color, p. 29*

Woman in Profile. 1937. Oil on canvas, 18½ x 11". The Phillips Gallery, Washington, D.C. *Ill. p. 99*

Children by the Road. 1938. Oil on canvas, 25 x 21¾". Lent by Jacques Guérin, Paris

Return from School after the Storm. 1939. Oil on canvas, 17 x 19½". The Phillips Gallery, Washington, D.C. *Ill. p 106*

Windy Day, Auxerre. 1939. Oil on canvas, 19¼ x 28⅜". The Phillips Gallery, Washington, D.C. *Ill. p. 104*

Maternity. 1942. Oil on canvas, 25½ x 20". Lent by M. and Mme Marcellin Castaing, Lèves, Eure-et-Loire, France. *Ill. p. 108*

Girl in Polka Dot Dress. 1942. Oil on canvas, 30¼ x 20⅛". Lent by Jacques Guérin, Paris. *Ill. p. 107*

Landscape with Reclining Figure. 1942. Oil on canvas, 28¼ x 35½". Lent by Jacques Guérin, Paris. *Ill. p. 109*

Autumn Trees, Champigny. 1942. Oil on canvas, 30¾ x 23¼". Lent by M. and Mme Marcellin Castaing, Lèves, Eure-et-Loire, France. *Ill. p. 110*

As this catalog goes to press, it is not certain that the paintings belonging to M. and Mme Marcellin Castaing can be included in the exhibition.

BIBLIOGRAPHY

Not included are references to newspaper articles; and references to books and periodicals in which only brief or insignificant mention is made of the artist. Exhibition catalogs, notices, and reviews are indicated in the "Exhibitions" section.

The following abbreviations have been used: Ap April, bibl. in this bibliography, col colored, D December, ed edition, F February, il illustration(s), Ja January, Je June, Jy July, Mr March, My May, N November, no number(s), O October, p page(s), pub. published.

For brevity, the designations *volume* and *page* have not been used in periodical references. Thus, the reference Amour de l'Art (Paris) 7no11:367–70 N 1926 means that the article may be found in volume 7, number 11, pages 367 to 370 of that magazine, published in Paris, in November 1926.

HANNAH B. MULLER
Assistant Librarian
The Museum of Modern Art

BOOKS AND ARTICLES

1 BAZIN, GERMAIN. Un nouveau fauvisme: Aujame. Amour de l'Art (Paris) 12:439–40 1931.
   Soutine and Aujame are compared.

2 BARNES, ALBERT C. Soutine. Arts à Paris (Paris) no10: 6–8 N 1924.

3 ——— The art in painting. 3d ed. p 374–5,383 il New York, Harcourt, Brace, 1937.
   ——— See also exhibition catalog, 1943, New York, Bignou Gallery.

4 CARCO, FRANCIS. L'ami des peintres. p46–7 Genève, Editions du Milieu du monde, 1944.

5 CHARENSOL, GEORGES. Soutine. Art Vivant (Paris) 3:547 1927.

6 COGNIAT, RAYMOND. Soutine. 37p plus plates (some col) Paris, Editions du Chêne, 1945.

7 COLLIÉ, ANDRÉE. Souvenirs sur Soutine. Spectateur des Arts (Paris) no1:14–18 D 1944.

   COLLIS, MAURICE. See exhibition catalog, 1947, London, Gimpel fils.

8 DORIVAL, BERNARD. Les étapes de la peinture française contemporaine. 3:187–93,197,199,200–5,207–8 Paris, Gallimard, 1946.

9 DOUGLAS, CHARLES. Artist quarter: reminiscences of Montmartre and Montparnasse. p316–20 et passim London, Faber and Faber, 1941.

10 DRIEU LA ROCHELLE, [PIERRE]. Soutine. il(some col) Formes (Paris) no5:4–5 My 1930.

11 EDOUARD-JOSEPH. Dictionnaire biographique des artistes contemporains, 1910–30. 3:310–11 il Paris, Librairie Grund, 1934.

12 ESCHOLIER, RAYMOND. La peinture française XXe siècle. p136,138 il Paris, Floury, 1937.

13 FAURE, ELIE. Soutine. 14p plus plates Paris, Crès, 1929. (Les Artistes nouveaux)
   Text reprinted with slight additions in the author's Ombres solides. p125–38 Paris, Société française d'éditions littéraires et techniques, 1934.

14 GAUNT, WILLIAM. The march of the moderns. p257 London, Jonathan Cape, 1949.

15 GEORGE, WALDEMAR. Soutine. il Amour de l'Art (Paris) 7no11:367–70 N 1926.

16 ——— Soutine. 23p plus plates Paris, Le Triangle, 1928. (Artistes juifs)

17 ——— Soutine et la violence dramatique. il Amour de l'Art (Paris) 14:150–2 1933.
Reprinted in bibl. 22.

18 GEORGES-MICHEL, MICHEL. Peintres et sculpteurs que j'ai connus, 1900–1942. p180–90 New York, Brentano's, 1942.

19 ——— Chefs d'oeuvre de peintres contemporains. p201, 203 il New York, Editions de la Maison française, 1945.
A poem.

——— See also exhibition catalog 1944, New York, Niveau Gallery.

20 GUILLAUME, PAUL. Soutine. Arts à Paris (Paris) no7:5–6 Ja 1923.

21 HISTORY OF MODERN PAINTING: MATISSE, MUNCH, ROUAULT, FAUVISM, EXPRESSIONISM. p122–9,145–6 col il Geneva, Albert Skira, 1950.

22 HUYGHE, RENÉ. Histoire de l'art contemporain, la peinture. p150–2 et passim il Paris, Alcan, 1935.
"Soutine et la violence dramatique, par Waldemar George" reprinted from bibl. 17. Biographical and bibliographical notes, p152.

23 LASSAIGNE, JACQUES. Cent chefs-d'oeuvre des peintres de l'Ecole de Paris. p104–6,119–21,200–1 il Paris, Editions de la Galerie Charpentier, 1947.
Text in French and English.

MCBRIDE, HENRY. See exhibition catalog, 1940, New York, Carroll Carstairs Gallery.

PARROT, LOUIS. See exhibition catalog, 1945, Paris, Galerie de France.

PHILLIPS, DUNCAN. See exhibition catalog, 1943, Washington, D.C., Phillips Memorial Gallery.

24 RAYNAL, MAURICE. Anthologie de la peinture en France de 1906 à nos jours. p287–90 il Paris, Editions Montaigne, 1927.
Translated into English in the author's Modern French painters. p151–2 il New York, Brentano's, 1928.

25 ——— Peintres du XXe siècle. p26–7 col il Genève, A. Skira, 1947.

26 SACHS, MAURICE. Soutine. il Creative Art (New York) 11no4:272–8 D 1932.

27 ——— Contre les peintres d'aujourd'hui. Nouvelle Revue Française (Paris) 43:28–42 Jy 1934.
Soutine, p39–40.

28 SAN LAZZARO, G. DI. Ricordo di Soutine. il Tre Arti (Milan) 1no1:8 1945.

29 "SIFRIAT POALIM" WORKER'S BOOK GUILD, TEL-AVIV. Amedeo Modigliani, Jules Pascin, Chaim Soutine. 8p plus plates Tel-Aviv, 1944.
Text in Hebrew.

30 SOBY, JAMES THRALL. Two painters of tragedy: Rouault and Soutine. In the author's Contemporary painters. p12–18 il New York, The Museum of Modern Art, 1948.

31 VENTURI, LIONELLO. Pittura contemporanea. p23 il Milano, U.Hoepli, 1947.

32 WHEELER, MONROE. 20th century portraits. p16,89 il New York, Museum of Modern Art, 1942.

33 WILENSKI, REGINALD H. Modern French painters. p80, 238,258,294,301,315,317 New York, Reynal & Hitchcock, 1940.
Later edition pub. 1944.

EXHIBITIONS: CATALOGS, REVIEWS

1927. Paris. Galerie Bing. June
For comment, see bibl. 5.

1930. Paris. Théâtre Pigalle. Group exhibition sponsored by "Art Vivant." May.
Reviewed in Art Vivant (Paris) 6no130:417,422,431 il My 15 1930. Includes biographical information.

1935. Chicago. Arts Club. December 13–30. 20 works.
Catalog with introduction by Edouard-Joseph, translated from bibl. 11.

1936. New York. Valentine Gallery. February 3–22. 21 works.
Catalog. Reviewed in Art News 34:5,7 F 8 1936; in Art Digest 10:12 F 15 1936.

1936. New York. Mrs. Cornelius J. Sullivan Gallery. February 24–March 15. 14 works.
Reviewed in Art News 34:10 Mr 7 1936.

1937. New York. Mrs. Cornelius J. Sullivan Gallery. March 22–April 17. 15 works.
Reviewed in Art News 35:14 Ap 10 1937; in Parnassus 9:44 Ap 1937.

1937. New York. Valentine Gallery. May 3–22.
Reviewed in Art Digest 11:20 My 15 1937; 11:22 Je 1937; in Art News 35:15 My 8 1937; in Magazine of Art 30:388–9 Je 1937.

1937. London. Leicester Galleries. April. 33 works.
Catalog with introduction by Maurice Sachs reprinted from bibl. 27, and biographical notes. Reviewed in Apollo 25:297 My 1937.

1937. Paris. Petit Palais. June–October. Group exhibition: Maîtres de l'Art Indépendant. 12 works.
Catalog.

1938. London. Storran Gallery. November. 12 works.

1939. New York. Valentine Gallery. March 20–April 8. 23 works.

Catalog. Reviewed in Art Digest 13:17 Ap 1 1939; in Art News 37:7 Mr 18 1939; in Parnassus 11:21–2 Ap 1939.

1940. New York. Carroll Carstairs Gallery. April 15–May 11. 12 works.

Catalog with introduction by Henry McBride. Reviewed in Art Digest 14:9 Ap 15 1940; in Parnassus 12:40 My 1940.

1943. Washington, D.C. Phillips Memorial Gallery. January 17–February 15. 23 works.

Catalog: Six loan exhibitions . . . with introduction by Duncan Phillips.

1943. New York. Bignou Gallery. March 22–April 16. 18 works.

Catalog with introduction by Albert C. Barnes. Reviewed in Art Digest 17:17 Ap 1 1943; in Art News 42: 23 Ap 1 1943.

1944. New York. Niveau Gallery. October 7–November 2. 13 works.

Catalog with introduction by Michel Georges-Michel. Reviewed in Art Digest 19:15 O 15 1944; in Art News 43:14 O 15 1944.

1944. Paris. Salon d'Automne.

Lamentable choice mentioned by Collié in bibl. 7. No listing in Salon catalog for that year.

1945. Paris. Galerie de France. January 12–end of February. 40 works.

Catalog with text by Louis Parrot. Reviewed in Arts (Paris) no1:1 Ja 31 1945.

1945. Boston. Institute of Modern Art. January 24–February 25. 22 works. (With Chagall.)

Catalog issued by United Modern Art in Boston: Art panorama.

1947. London. Gimpel fils. April 23–May 17. 18 works.

Catalog with introduction by Maurice Collis.

1947. Paris. Galerie Zak. November 29–December 31. 19 works.

No catalog. Reviewed in Arts (Paris) no143:2 D 5 1947; in Panorama des arts, 1947. p239–41 Paris, Somogy, 1948; in Kroniek van Kunst en Kultuur (Amsterdam) 9no2:64 F 1948.

1949. New York. Van-Diemen-Lilienfeld Galleries. January 5–20. 7 works. (With Utrillo.)

Catalog. Reviewed in Art Digest 23:14 Ja 15 1949.

THIS REPRINTED EDITION WAS PRODUCED BY THE OFFSET PRINTING PROCESS. THE TEXT AND PLATES WERE PHOTOGRAPHED SEPARATELY FROM THE ORIGINAL VOLUME, AND THE PLATES RESCREENED. THE PAPER AND BINDING WERE SELECTED TO ENSURE THE LONG LIFE OF THIS LIBRARY GRADE EDITION.